WORKING WITH PEOPLE

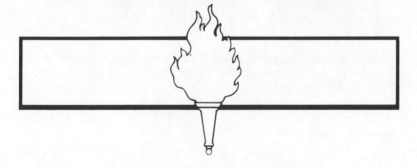

Doran C. McCarty

BROADMAN PRESS
Nashville, Tennessee

Unless otherwise stated, all Scripture quotations are from the Revised Standard·
Version of the Bible, copyrighted 1946, 1952, © 1971, 1973.

Scripture quotations marked KJV are from the King James Version of the Bible.

Scripture quotations marked GNB are from the *Good News Bible,* the Bible in Today's English Version. Old Testament: Copyright © American Bible Society 1976;
New Testament: Copyright © American Bible Society 1966, 1971, 1976. Used by
permission.

Scripture quotations marked Moffatt are from *The Bible: a New Translation* by James
A. R. Moffatt. Copyright © 1935 by Harper and Row, Publishers, Inc. Used by
permission.

Scripture quotations marked NASB are from the *New American Standard Bible.*
Copyright © The Lockman Foundation. 1960, 1962, 1963, 1968, 1971, 1972, 1973,
1975, 1977. Used by permission.

Library of Congress Cataloging-in-Publication Data

McCarty, Doran.
    Working with people.

    (Broadman leadership series)
    1. Church management.   2. Interpersonal relations—
Religious aspects—Christianity.   I. Title.
II. Series.
BV652.9.M36   1987   253   86-17573

This book is dedicated to my four
daughters:
Gaye Lynn, Risë Kay, Marletta Jean
and Leslie Beth.
From their infancy to their adulthood,
they have helped me grow in love,
concern, and grace.

Contents

Preface 7

1. God with Us—A Model for Relationships 9

2. But I Can't Get Along with 12

3. Levels of Relationships 23

4. Clues About How You Relate 37

5. A Supporting Cast 57

6. Working with a Staff 67

7. Working with Volunteers 99

8. Confrontation 107

Epilogue 124

Bibliography 125

Preface

The Broadman Leadership Series seeks to help ministers to become more effective leaders. Some of the tasks of ministers are more human or divine, more organizational or personal. This book seeks to integrate the various polarities.

Scripture emphasizes both the kingdom of God and concern for people. These are not artificial, but are grounded in the nature of reality and humanity.

Management has become a major area of study in the United States. By observing people, management experts have developed some management processes which are consistent with biblical principles of human relations. This book seeks to integrate the best of management concepts with the gospel function of a minister-leader. Management principles do not replace the gospel, but at times provide help in understanding how to translate gospel truth into functioning ministry.

God cares for people. May we ministers always be alert to find ways to make the love and concern we preach on Sunday work for us as leaders during the week.

The message of this book is that if we take care of people, we will get our work done more effectively. We are not only in the business of getting things done but also of growing people. Effective leaders live with this polarity.

I owe thanks to many, especially Kristi Niece, my secretary, and Elizabeth Meloney and her angels in Secretarial Services.

1
God with Us—A Model for Relationships

Wayne Ward relates that on one of his trips to the Holy Land, a Moslem guide said to him, "Our religions aren't so different. We believe in Allah and you in God; we believe Mohammed was a prophet and you believe Jesus was a prophet." Ward responded that Christians believe that Jesus was God incarnated as a man. The Moslem guide looked at Ward in disbelief as though Ward had struck him. The next day the Moslem guide found Ward and told him, "I've been talking to others and they tell me that Christians do believe that Jesus was God. If it could only be true; if it would only be true."

Of course it is true—Jesus was God incarnate. The word *Immanuel* means "God with us." While there are important theological implications to "God with us," this is also a model for human relationships. God chose to come as a man and identify with the plight of humanity and "has in every respect been tempted as we are" (Heb. 4:15). God came in Jesus and "dwelt among us" (John 1:14). He pitched His tent in our camp. As one expressed it, "He made the scene with us." (The word for "dwelled" in Greek, *skene*, transliterates into "scene.")

You relate to people by being with them as Jesus did. You understand and appreciate them by walking with them and understanding their pilgrimages. An American Indian adage says not to criticize a man until you've walked a mile in his moccasins.

I met with the Doctor of Ministry supervisors one fall to plan the year's work and tell them about the new doctoral candidates. When I mentioned one new candidate, moans went up from each one who knew him. They asked why we had let him in the program. Although the new candidate was a bright young man, they didn't like him. I passed around the young man's life history for the supervisors to read. When they finished, there were tears in their eyes. They said that they had never known about his unfortunate childhood and they wanted to know how they could help. Most of the supervisors had occasions to work with the new doctoral candidate and went out of their way to help him. There were few supervisors' meetings that someone did not ask how the new candidate was doing. They understood him. There is a different story about the doctor who stood on the deck of his ship and, using a telescope, tried to diagnose the sailors on another ship who were ill. He was afraid to expose himself by getting too close to them. How unlike Immanuel that is—God with us!

When God chose to reveal Himself most fully, it was personal—His personal presence in Jesus Christ. His fullest revelation was not a book, an angel, a sermon, or a song but the blessed advent of Immanuel. He walked in the midst of humanity, giving the best of heaven and receiving the worst of the world. Deism is the belief that God is aloof from the world like a watchmaker who makes a fine instrument, then lays it down to run on while he goes elsewhere. That was not the God of Jesus Christ, Immanuel—God *with* us.

A major problem in human relations is our inability with intimacy. Behind this problem is our difficulty in revealing ourselves to others. We withdraw behind masks of roles and rules. Jesus cherished roles and rules but only as a means to guard the integrity of relationships. He did not come to hide God but to reveal Him. He did not observe us from a nearby planet but came as Immanuel—God with us. He walked the dusty roads of the Holy Land alongside other men with hurting feet who needed them bathed. He walked through golden fields and, with other hungry men, rubbed the grain in His hands to gain sustenance. He went with them to their wedding feasts and synagogues. He wept with them before the tombs of loved ones. He was "God with us."

Jesus came and took the servant role among us. He dramatically acted this out during the Last Supper when He washed the feet of His disciples. Jesus said many things, but one which stuck with the disciples was that He ". . . came not to be served but to serve" (Matt. 20:28). The apostle Paul offered a great hymn to the Philippian church:

"Have this mind among yourselves, which is yours in Christ Jesus, who, though he was in the form of God, did not count equality with God a thing to be grasped, but emptied himself, taking the form of a servant, being born in the likeness of men" (Phil. 2:5-7).

Recently I attended a Fred Pryor Seminar for managers. The group was made up of presidents of schools and corporate managers. The eloquent speaker spent the day telling his audience how to be better managers. Toward the end of the day the speaker told the group that if they really wanted to be effective managers, they would have to become servants.

Robert Greenleaf has written a book which has become popular. The title is *Servant Leadership*[1] and the subtitle is, "A Journey into the Nature of Legitimate Power and Greatness." Greenleaf spent many years with A.T. & T. before his retirement. His philosophy is, "But to me . . . *the great leader is seen as servant first,* and that simple fact is the key to his greatness."[2]

Being an effective leader and relating to people effectively depends upon our service. Immanuel taught us that, and the best minds of management understand that. There are many heroes of faith in Christian history who demonstrated it—Francis of Assisi, Martin Luther, William Carey, Bill Wallace, and Albert Schweitzer are among the servants.

Immanuel blessed us. *God with us* was the supreme blessing of history. We give blessings to others by our presence. It isn't enough for a presidential candidate to appear on television and give out press reports. Cities vie for a candidate to visit their communities. Pastors know the elation of driving in front of a home and hearing an ecstatic child run into the house yelling, "The preacher's here." As with Immanuel, loving presence is important.

Notes

1. Robert K. Greenleaf, *Servant Leadership* (New York: Paulist Press, 1977), p. 335.

2. Ibid., p. 7.

2
But I Can't Get Along with . . .

"I'm going to resign next week even though I don't have any other place to go. I just can't get along with the pastor." Jim Walters* told this to the small group in the seminar I conducted. He had been minister of music for eighteen months at the church.

Jim Walters' story is not new. Most of us have heard it from others and perhaps even said it. If we haven't had this experience in our vocation, we have said, "but I can't get along with . . ." about others. There are people it seems impossible to get along with—or for *us* to get along with. Perhaps we need to recognize our limitations. The fact is, we won't be able to get along with everyone. We can get along with Jim, John, Jane, and Julie, but not with Jack. We wonder what is wrong with Jack. After a while we begin to have self-doubts and wonder what is wrong with us. We may begin to wonder if things are really so good between ourselves and Jim, John, June, and Julie.

One of the myths we live with is that we ought to be able to get along with everybody. Ideally that may be right, but it doesn't work that way. The myth makes us feel guilty and the guilt may erode our relationships with others. If I were perfect and lived in a perfect world, perhaps I would be able to get along with everyone. Neither I nor the world is perfect.

Paul's Advice

After having said, "Live in harmony with one another" (Rom. 12:16), Paul spoke to the reality we all face: "If possible, so far as it depends upon you, live peaceably with all" (v. 18).

We need to enter the precious world of personal relationships

*This name and those in other illustrations are not the real names.

dressed with the desire and determination to "live peaceably with all" but also wise enough to know we can't. After all, Paul had enemies and ended up beaten, imprisoned, and thrown out of synagogues. He didn't always get along with some of his Christian brethren—Simon Peter, John Mark, Barnabas. And God has His Satan.

Why Can't We Get Along?

Karen, a teenager, burst into the living room of the home where I was making a pastoral visit and haughtily proclaimed, "I never want to see Cliff again. I don't like him. I never liked him. And I'll never like him." Because I was interim pastor, I didn't get to see how that turned out. You have heard adolescents express absolute vehemence about a peer. Adults may be more restrained in expressing their dislike for others, but the reality is that adults can't get along with everybody.

Do We Want To?

Why can't we get along with others? One thing I was slow to learn counseling with couples with critical marital problems was to ask, "Do you want to stay married?" For a long time I assumed every couple who came to me wanted to stay married. I do. Christians should. I found out that not everyone wants to stay married. Why can't we get along with others? The first question we need to ask is, "Do we want to get along with others?" A couple of friends told me what an ogre Reverend Bryan was. I had never met Bryan but I knew what school he had gone to and that was bad news in my book. He had invited people I didn't admire to speak in his church. He had fired a friend of mine who was on the staff when he went to his present pastorate. Prepared with all these negative feelings, we were about to serve on a committee together where we would meet for the first time. I knew I wasn't going to like him. I wasn't going to get along with him. I was going to oppose his ideas in the committee. I didn't want to get along with him.

Does that story seem familiar? I think most of us have had experiences where we didn't intend to get along with others even if we didn't say it out loud or admit it to ourselves. We have felt that way about ministers, community people, and those who married into our family. Reverend Bryan and I met at our first committee meeting. When I was introduced to him, he told me what great things he had heard about what I was doing at the seminary and if he could ever help me, let him know. During the committee meeting, I found that we agreed on far more things than we disagreed. And I had come prepared not to work with him. I am grateful that he was more gracious than I.

Great Expectations

We may not get along with others because of our expectations. Our wives don't do for us as our mothers. Professors don't take care of us as our fathers. Church members don't have the same ideas as our fellow ministers. America has been diagnosed as being in a narcissistic era. People captured by inordinate self-love demand more than they can consistently extract from others.

Responding to Our Past

His jaw jutted out. His lips were tight. His words were clipped and precise as he made his point. I felt like a little boy. I felt steam building inside. Suddenly, I became aware of my increasing blood pressure and asked myself what was going on. Sitting reflectively for a moment, I became aware how much the speaker was like my father when he was angry at me. The speaker was not even addressing me, but he had made me feel like a resentful little boy, bringing back emotions out of my childhood. I wonder how many times I have responded to my past rather than the situation in which I was engaged.

Therapists who developed Transactional Analysis created a model for discussing events such as I experienced. People store their experiences in their minds the way we record music on tape. We may not remember events consciously but they are always there, ready to play again. When an event happens to us similar to one from the past, or a voice sounds like one out of our past, or someone looks like someone we interacted with in the past, we replay those old tapes. We may not "remember" the situations or words but we react emotionally as we did in the past. Sometimes there is no logical reason for us not to like or work with another person. Your spouse, secretary, and friends get along with the person, but you can't because the person is triggering your old tapes.

When we are trapped by our past, we need to get in charge of our lives and relating. We may be letting the fifth-grade bully or the bossy neighbor of our childhood determine present interactions with people.

Under What Circumstances?

News spread around the small town quickly—Lola had attacked some of her high school classmates. Not much damage except a few scratches and sore heads where hair had been pulled. Her friends reported that no one could get along with Lola the last few weeks. That was only days before Lola and her boyfriend were visiting me, asking that I marry them. Lola was pregnant.

We do not relate and work with people in a vacuum. People are not machines brought to work in a bus to be plugged in at 8:00 AM and unplugged at 4 PM. People come as persons and bring their circumstances with them—family, financial, emotional, and health circumstances. Physical exhaustion lowers inhibitions and energy has to be used to focus and remain conscious. One Sunday I preached at morning and evening services of a church, caught a 1:00 AM plane, which skipped through the South like a flat rock thrown on a lake, and ended up on the East Coast at 8:15 AM, where I was to speak and relate to the youth at 9:00 AM. Disaster!

People live in the circumstances of fear, hurt, illness, and crises. Joann had been through a divorce. Joann's husband had left her and their two boys and was living in a homosexual relationship. Joann no longer attended church or her sons' school activities. Absenteeism at work was a problem. She had difficulty even going to the store for groceries. Joann's assessment was, "I feel like I've had the rug pulled out from under me and I don't feel like anyone or anything has meaning for me anymore. I shared years with a man who hurt me so deeply."

Personal Patterns

People are as different as their unique, individual fingerprints. Recently the city of San Francisco paid more than a million dollars for a computer to check fingerprints. This is possible because there are classes of fingerprints. Although people are as unique as the fabled snowflakes, there are personality patterns. These patterns provide some of the answers as to why we can't get along with some people.

One year another director of field education and I had a planning assignment for a meeting. I noticed each time I met with him that, after a few minutes, I was irritable and resentful. My first hunch was that he didn't like Baptists but, as I listened, I found no reason for that judgment. My next hunch was that he didn't like Midwesterners, but that didn't wash. (Notice I thought the problem was his, not mine.) Having been active in leading Bi-Polar Seminars,[1] I decided to analyze the situation with that tool. I found the problem—we were alike! Our personalities had the same pattern. While I admired the man for what he accomplished, working with him was difficult.

People with different patterns may have difficulty working together. According to some research I've read, 80 percent of all ministers fall into two patterns out of a possible sixteen patterns while 95 percent of managers fall into two different categories. I have no doubt that difference relates to many of the serious conflicts ministers are experiencing in churches. Laypersons complain about a minister's lack of personal relating skills and that they can't work with him. Personality patterns make a difference. (For more on this, see the chapter "Clues to How You Relate.")

Whose Goals?

A group of horse-farm owners in the bluegrass country of Kentucky reportedly asked for a meeting with the owner of a large and prosperous horse farm. The small farm owners were having difficulty competing with the multi-million-dollar farm syndicate. The wealthy owner of the syndicate asked the neighboring farmers: "Are you in this business to make money?" When they answered affirmatively, the wealthy owner replied, "That's the problem; I'm in this business to spend money." They left without resolving their problems—one with a goal to spend money, others with the goal to make money.

People must have some compatible goals if they relate and work together effectively. Conflicting goals cause clashes like trying to put a car in gear without using the clutch. Things don't mesh. Whether persons are in a marriage, a company, or a church, they will have to have compatible goals to work together very long.

We may be able to work with people on particular projects where we have a common goal although our broad-based goals conflict. (I am reminded of the strange alliance between our American government and some foreign dictators to whom we give military and economic aid.) To be effective, we have to work with people who share our goals on projects even if our goals otherwise are disparate. Sometimes we do this in a symbiotic way. Private utility companies exist for profit; churches exist for service. When the church uses utilities, each group reaches their goals, even if they are different.

Working as a Team

We have to get along as a team, don't we? Wrong! Many teams never mesh and limp through their assignments. Each reason given in this chapter could be the reason people on a particular team can't work together. Unless one person or a group within the team takes over and does the team's work, the team will have to learn to work together. The longer the term of service, the more important it is to work together. A committee to decorate for a party may get a job done in spite of the problems, but a church staff is a different matter.

Team building goes through developmental stages. Relational difficulties is the mark of one of those stages. Why can't we work harmoniously all the time? Because one stage in team building elicits conflict. Charles Keating cites five stages in team building: Polite, Purpose, Power, Constructive, and Esprit. In Keating's stages, difficulty arises normally in the power stage.[2] Another model has four stages: forming, norming, storming, and performing.[3] You have to go through the difficult stage of storming and power, but you don't have to get locked into it. When new people form the team, you go back to the beginning of the process because a new person means a new team. When a person joins a team which has been together a long time, the new person may not be given the freedom to "storm" and may never "join the team."

Values Make a Difference

Getting along with people depends on having compatible values. People who grow up in the same family and community tend to have like values. There are, however, many values in any community, even if some are more recessive. An urban community is so pluralistic that the whole range of human values can be found, not only the dominant ones. While we may not lose values we form in early life, we may shift our value emphasis as a result of circumstances, education, vocation, or friends. Since our major values are often held with a sense of absolutism, we may have problems working with people who have our primary values as their secondary values.

Those Crazy People

My family was not part of the aristocratic, landed gentry of the old South but people from the foothills of the Ozarks with a simple life-style and plain ways. When I preached in the South one week, I stayed in a Southern colonial-style home with a judge and his family who were Southern patricians. While our values were basically the same, our life-styles were very different. A professor and entertainer or a pastor and physician may have differing life-styles, causing one or both to be threatened (or jealous). Trouble accelerates when people defend life-styles as though they were values.

Residents in a small town were up by 5:30 AM to go to the field or to commute to the city to work. They insisted that any church committee meeting be over before 9:00 PM because they had to be to bed by 10:00 PM. The pastor usually read and worked on sermons until after midnight and didn't get up until nearly 8:00 AM. His parishioners had trouble with the pastor's life-style. Some parishioners accused him of being lazy and others thought he was too "citified."

Roy Boatright was one of my models for ministry when I was a young minister. (He retired after serving as director of Sunday School work for Kentucky Baptists for many years.) I had the good fortune of being the pastor of Jameson Baptist Church in Jameson, Missouri, years after Roy had an excellent ministry there. The people told me that Roy was up before 6:00 AM every morning and by 7:00 AM, he was down at the store operated by a deacon, visiting with people as they came through. They said that by 9:00 or 10:00 AM he had visited everyone in town. I often wondered what Roy did the rest of the day. It didn't matter. He had adopted the people's life-style and that was one of the reasons Roy got along with people in the church so well.

Games People Play

Eric Berne has made famous the idea of game playing in human relations.[4] Games get in the way of relationships and keep us from revealing ourselves to others. It is difficult to work with someone who plays games. Much time and energy are required to play the games or to get behind the games to what is really going on with the persons. While game players may be neurotic, healthier people also resort to games so people can't get too close to them or at least not too close too soon. Game players may not intend to be dishonest, but they don't know how to relate in a straightforward way or are afraid of getting hurt or of not measuring up.

Prejudice

I held a revival meeting—or rather preached a week—in the South where there was deep racial prejudice. There was no way there could have been an effective evangelistic effort because the people were too distracted. Since it was during the mid-1960s when racial turmoil was great, feelings ran high. Every time someone opened the church door, the congregation turned around and looked in fear that a black would come into the auditorium. One deacon, otherwise not unmarked by saintliness, said to me, "They have their own church; I don't know why they would want to come to ours."

All prejudice isn't racial. There is prejudice against women, people of differing religions, life-styles, politics, education, and economic or social status. While prejudice may be overcome after a long period of time and probably agony, it hinders personal and working relationships.

Alternatives in Getting Along

Accept reality. It doesn't help to wish that people or you were different. The reality is that we live in a world with human relations problems. Wars, feuds, and church splits testify to that reality. Accepting the reality of problems doesn't mean doing nothing about them. In fact, we will respond. The question is, "Will we choose the best alternative?"

Each person has a different pain threshold. Some can stand more physical pain than others, and the same is true with psychic pain. When people can't get along, there will be psychic pain. Before we can determine the proper alternative, we need to look at the pain involved in each alternative and determine our tolerance level. Perhaps the ideal would be to try to redeem a situation and bring about reconciliation, but we may not be able to cope with the stress.

Two professors were having lunch. One would soon leave the school for another position. The two professors had disagreed strongly for a number of years in faculty and committee meetings. One professor said, "I'm sorry you're leaving. We've disagreed many times but I never felt you treated me with disrespect or lack of integrity."

Most people act out of the best judgment they have. Just because we can't get along doesn't mean that the other person is less concerned for the good of a church or people than we are. They see things differently and do things differently. People will forgive us of nearly anything if we treat them with respect and integrity. Our friends will become nervous about us and not support us if we don't treat others with respect and integrity.

Survival

A course we ought to teach in seminaries is "How to Survive." Too many ministers don't survive long enough in a church to deal with their problems creatively and redemptively. If you plan to stay at a place a long time, getting along with people is your most important achievement. If you are going to be at a church twenty years, relating and working with the people is more important than remodeling or dividing Sunday School classes.

Survival isn't as simple as saying, "I'm going to survive!" The official structure of an organization dictates part of the survival technique, as does environment. This means learning the formal and informal rules and living within them until they can be improved. Usually someone else will have to take the initiative to change the rules and you will have the role of blessing the change.

Survival is important for another reason. Being with people may bring intimacy after a long period of time even if you can't get along during that time. Where there is integrity and respect, intimacy can grow in the midst of conflict.

Flee

Jim Walters (mentioned at the beginning of this chapter) planned to resign without a place to go, just to get away. Fleeing was the only option he knew. He had no support system to help him find and sort out options. There are times to flee. When you reach your tolerance level, you need to flee, unless what you are working with is such a moral issue for the world that you feel called to martyrdom.

Avoid

When you can't get along with someone, you may avoid him. A pastor loves to visit some parishioners but avoids others. He visits them only when there is a crisis. While nothing redemptive is likely with that behavior, a person may not be able to tolerate more.

Limited Relationship

You may be able to work with a person in a structured relationship (such as a committee meeting) but have difficulties getting along with the person in a nonstructured situation. Your response may be to establish a limited relationship.

Developing a Relationship

Larry, a pastor of a new mission church, told some of his peers about his experience with the pastor of the sponsoring church. Larry explained that they had difficulties from the beginning and that he couldn't get along with the pastor. Larry said, "I knew I was going to have to work with him a long time, so I decided to try to build a working relationship. I went to his office and asked him to tell me about how he got to be pastor of the church, what he was happy about in the church, and what his dreams were. I was prepared to keep going back until things changed but they really thawed that first time. We had prayer together before we left and we've gotten along well since."

The most productive response is to develop a relationship with people with whom you have difficulties. Like Larry, you need to prepare to invest a great deal of time and energy in developing the relationship. It takes a long time to build a cathedral and it must be built stone by stone. Relationships develop a step at a time. Each step of progress has to be earned—there is no magic.

Notes

1. Bi-Polar Seminars were developed by Dr. J. W. Thomas. For more information write Bi-Polar Inc., P. O. Box 1237, Richardson, Texas, 75080.

2. Charles Keating, *Dealing with Difficult People* (Ramsey, N. J.: Paulist Press, 1984), p. 15f.

3. E. Mansell Pattison, *Pastor and Parish—A Systems Approach* (Philadelphia: Fortress Press, 1977), pp. 59-60.

4. Eric Berne, *Games People Play* (New York: Grove Press, 1964), p. 192.

3
Levels of Relationships

I was leading a supervision seminar at a college when I mentioned that there was a limit to how many people with whom I could be close. One minister took exception to the idea. After an energetic response, he ended by saying, "The Bible says that 'God so loved the world.'" My only possible response was, "But I'm not God."

Unless I am messianic, I have to admit that I can be close to a few and have other relationships of varying intensities. I have said facetiously (I hope) that God loves all, I tolerate some. Each of us has only so much time and psychic energy. Relationships consume both. It takes an omnipotent God to be omnipresent. (I tend to dislike absolute, abstract Latin terms, but maybe they communicate in this situation.) In our human, mutual frailty, we have limited time and energy which means a limitation on relationships. Since that is a reality we live with, we need to be purposeful in developing appropriate, meaningful relationships. By "appropriate" I mean that we need to have relationships on several levels and recognize that each level of relationship has its own meaning.

Jesus' Levels of Relationships

Jesus demonstrated levels of relationships. He had a special intimacy with the twelve disciples. One might argue that even among those there was an inner circle of Peter, James, and John, although it is not beyond dispute that their special place might have been due to a special status rather than intimacy. In the Gospel of John, chapters 13—17, we have a picture of Jesus' special affection for the twelve. The story of Lazarus in John 11 shows us some of Jesus' special intimates. There was a different level of relationship with the multitudes in the story of feeding the 5,000 (Matt. 14). Matthew reports that after the feeding of the multitude, Jesus dismissed the crowd and had the disciples board a boat, and He met them later.

One of the most amazing things about Jesus was His relationship with women—unusual for any man, especially a man in His day. The Gospels record many occasions of Jesus relating with spiritual intensity with women. The story of the woman at the well preserves the manner with which Jesus was able to get behind the mask and reserve to an open and sensitive interaction. Although there is a large body of literature by and reflecting Paul, it does not show the same relationships to women as shown in the life of Jesus!

Jesus related to people at different levels: family, disciples, intimates, the public, and distractors. He related individually, in small groups, and in massive crowds.

Keeping People at a Distance

A common but trivial problem in developing relationships at any level is our inability to be transparent to people. We keep people at a distance. Rather than connecting with people, we keep them away by using masks and games. Of course we don't begin relating with full-blown relationships. There is a "courtship" in which we explore the new island of another person.

Life has been described as a costume ball where participants dress in costumes and masks to hide their identity. Little by little, friends begin to recognize one another. Life has at least one difference; everyone doesn't take off their masks at midnight. We may become comfortable with our masks and always wear them. We meet with people but protect ourselves because, as Alan McGinnis puts it, "We long both to be known and to remain hidden."[1]

Why do we "need" masks? There is what the Swiss psychoanalyst Carl Jung called the shadow side of our personality. We are reluctant to expose the shadow side to others. The shadow side of us is made up of our feelings of guilt, shame, fear, and inadequacy. Self-disclosure of our shadow side risks rejection.

Masks make it difficult to develop relationships with people because we are forced to interact with the mask rather than the person. We may further confuse others by changing masks and, like the television game show, cause others to ask, "Will the real person stand up?" The mask wearer can hide behind the mask so long and tenaciously that he or she "forgets" the real identity. The primitive man, looking in a mirror for the first time, may be puzzled because he has never seen that face before. If we rely extensively on masks, we become hollow underneath—as though it were a death mask on a corpse, and all that's left is the mask since the body has decayed away.

There are many masks. The following list may help identify some masks we've experienced (or used).

Wisdom—People like to appear wise rather than stupid. We may flaunt our education, groups of facts, or definitive judgments in using this mask. (The most successful usually use a lot of silence.)

Sophistication—This social game employs name dropping, tales of world travel, dress, and tastes in "wine, women, and song"—and even theology.

Piousity—While piousity (not piety) is usually a mask of the religious or would-be religious, it has at least two other forms. There is a reverse kind of piousity in acting out antipiousness. Rather than saying that one is better because of piousity, a person says that one is better because of not being pious. Also there are "causes" which create the same kind of piousity as traditional religion.

Innocence—By speaking of the mask of innocence, I don't mean to imply that the wearer is any more guilty than the next person. The mask of innocence, worn well, makes the wearer less vulnerable immediately, but people may feel dreadfully betrayed by any deviate behavior. The mask of innocence may arouse unfounded suspicions in others.

Naiveté—"The poor, sweet, little, helpless thing" is universally recognized as a ploy, but it may hide the real person behind the mask.

Clown—Phyllis Diller and Erma Bombeck may be funny entertainers, but their clowning carried into the social arena can thwart genuine relationships.

Lover—This person may try the Romeo lover's mask or the mask of saccharine sentimentality.

Naughty/Rascal—The woman may wear the naughty mask and the man the rascal mask. Whatever they do, they have nothing to live down.

Brute—This may be the "macho" man or the "tough guy at the office."

Cutting the Distance
Between Others and Ourselves

If I become able to relate without depending on masks, I will need to develop transparency. No one can make me become transparent; I have to work on it myself. Sidney Jourard says, "There's no way to force somebody to talk about himself. You can only invite."[2] If I wish to become transparent, I must ask a question about myself: "Can I tolerate the nakedness of relating without a mask?" Cultural mores, family background, and the reinforcement of life's experience make it very difficult for some of us to be vulnerable to others. Also, I must ask two questions of the person to whom I wish to relate. First, can he or she stand to see me in my nakedness without my mask? Second, can I hope to trust them if I make myself vulnerable and don't wear my mask?

Let me suggest four things which will help develop transparency and make relationships better. First, tell the person how you feel about him or her. As a youngster I heard someone say, "I wish I had told him how I felt about him before he died." That stuck with me. Why hadn't she? Yet I find myself not letting people know how I feel about them. I recall when a friend looked at me intensely and said, "Doran, I love you." I don't remember a man ever saying that to me before. His confession of feeling deeply affected me, how I relate to him, and what I share with him.

Second, tell what you hope. A friend of mine resisted this because, as he said, then you would know whether I lived up to it or not. You risk making a fool of yourself or a friend of the other person.

Third, tell what you fear. Once you name a demon, you can more nearly drive him out.

Fourth, tell about your hurts. Resist the temptation to "bear your cross alone." Sharing hurts helps you get in touch with them so you can build a bridge to another person rather than letting hurts separate you.

We are not only made in the image of God; we do possess a "shadow side." We need to be in touch with that shadow side of life and own it. When we reveal ourselves to others without masks, we move toward being the full person God intended for us to be.

Models to Understand Our Relating

Some models have been developed which help us visualize our levels of relationships. In 1955 Joe Luft and Harry Ingham presented a model (which has become known as the Johari Window) to help interpret relationships. Luft draws the model which follows:[3]

The Johari Window

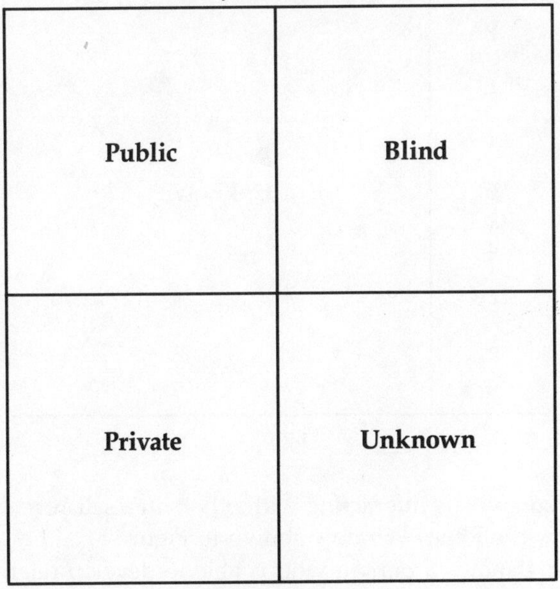

Public	**Blind**
Private	**Unknown**

Figure 1

Dr. Robert Dale interprets the Johari Window as follows:

Quadrant 1 is the "Open Me." It displays behavior and motivation known to others and me.

Quadrant 2 is the "Blind Me." It is the area of activity others see in me—but I'm unaware of my behavior at this point. The Pharisees of Matthew 23 are examples of this kind of behavior.

Quadrant 3 is the "Hidden Me." It represents items I know about myself but do not reveal to others.

Quadrant 4 is the "Unknown Me." It points to areas of my life of which neither others nor myself have any degree of awareness.[4]

A person who depends on masks to hide from others may have a personal Johari Window that looks like Figure 2.

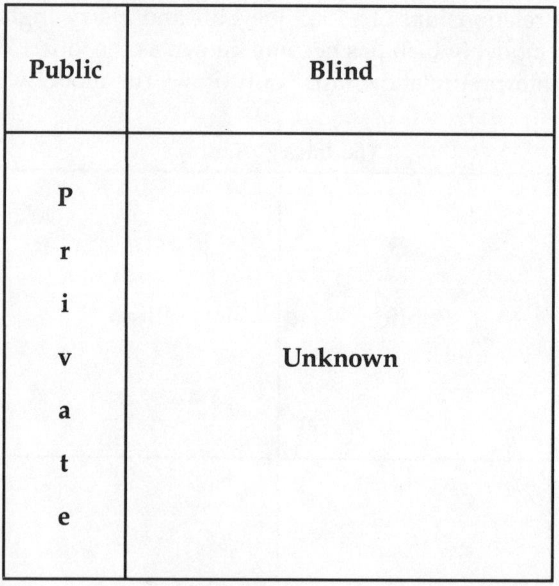

Public	Blind
P r i v a t e	Unknown

Figure 2

A person who is interacting with others in a self-revealing way may have the Johari Window shown in Figure 3.

Figure 4 shows a person who is able to develop relationships and get close to a number of people. This happens when the person is able to risk self-disclosure and feedback.

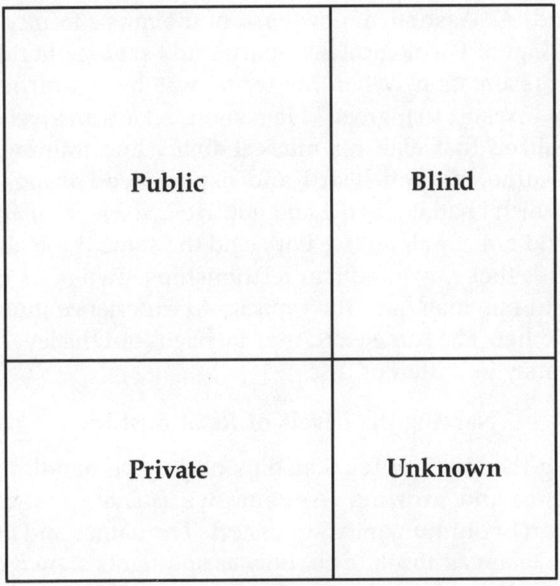

Public	**Blind**
Private	**Unknown**

Figure 3

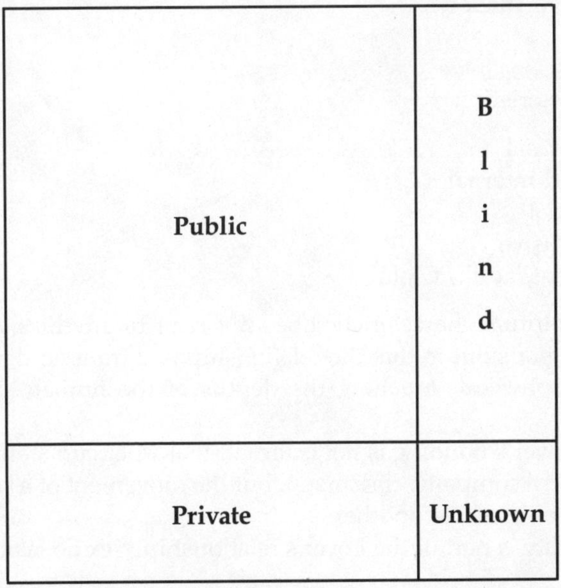

Public	**B** **l** **i** **n** **d**
Private	**Unknown**

Figure 4

A friend, Al Washburn, now head of the music faculty at New Orleans Baptist Theological Seminary, and I sat together during a musical presentation. When the recital was over, I turned to Al and said, "Wasn't that great!" He responded affirmatively. I suddenly realized that with his musical ability and training far exceeding mine, he had heard and experienced things in the concert which I had not and could not. He had a level of appreciation I could not equal, but we both said the same thing about the concert. It's that way in human relationships. Two of us may say "love," but one may have the capacity to experience much more than the other. The same word may be used, but the level of relationship may be different.

Naming the Levels of Relationships

Naming the levels of relationships helps give handles for understanding and growing. Anytime we isolate, analyze, and name a part of our humanity, we distort. The names and analyses cannot be taken as absolute but only as spotlights shown on relationships to help us see them more clearly even though the lights also create shadows.

Lover

Characteristics:

Spiritual
Bond internal
Sexual
Exclusive
Parent, adult, Child

The spiritual characteristic does not refer to anything specifically religious but to that the relationship that transcends the social and physical, touching the depths of the human spirit or soul.

The Lover's bonding is not external, that is, circumstantial (coworker in a company, classmate), but the movement of a free person reaching out to another.

Sexuality is part of the Lover's relationship. Sex does not guarantee a close and intimate relationship, but it has the capacity to deepen the relationship and make it more intimate.

The Lover's relationship is exclusive. It is difficult if not impossible for the Lover's level relationship to include more than the primary couple.

Transactional Analysis provides the terminology of parent, adult, and child. Muriel James and Dorothy Jongeward say that "the *Parent ego state* contains the attitudes and behavior incorporated from external sources, primarily parents."[5] The parent ego state is marked by "oughtness," either oughtness on oneself to help others (nurturing) or oughtness imposed on others (critical and judgmental). They said that the "*Adult ego state* is not related to a person's age. It is oriented to current reality and the objective gathering of information."[6] This is computerlike, cognitive data. They explain that the "*Adult ego state* contains all the impulses that come naturally to an infant."[7] This ego state can be seen in rebellion, playfulness, creativity, and imagination.

I have capitalized the Parent and Child to indicate that I believe they have a major role in the Lover's level of relating. Lovers nurture one another (Parent) and enjoy and play (Child). There will need to be some adult (therefore the small "a") in a responsible Lover's level of relationships. When the relationship loses the Parent and the Child and becomes too invested in the adult, people lose the spark of their romance.

Intimate

Characteristics:

Spiritual
Bond-internal
Nonsexual
Semiexclusive
Parent, adult, Child

The spiritual, bonding, and transactional characteristics of intimates are the same as Lovers. The Intimates are nonsexual, although sex may be a temptation and sexual feelings may be beneath the surface. The Intimate relationship is usually semiexclusive because most people have more than one Intimate. Very possessive people may have difficulty as an Intimate when they demand exclusiveness.

Friend

Characteristics:

Bond-internal
Nonsexual
Semiinclusive
Parent, adult, Child

While the spiritual element may be emerging at the Friend level, it is not yet formed. The relationship is semiinclusive. A person has numerous friends but does not make friendships indiscriminately, hence they are *semi*inclusive.

Partner

Characteristics:

Bond-external
Nonsexual
Semiinclusive
Parent, Adult, child

The bond at the Partner level is external as it comes from the job, task, or common activity. According to the Clinebells, crises or conflicts may be the external bonds.[8] There is a shift in the ego states most frequently used. Partners have a task to do in the present, so they tend to be in the Adult ego state more. If they operate in the parent or Child ego state much, they will jeopardize the partner relationship. Good and productive partnerships will have times of taking care of the needs of others and joyful, celebrative moments.

Companion

Characteristics:

Bond-external
Nonsexual

Semiinclusive
Parent, adult, child

Imagine a carpool. The bond is external and exists because they are together. Presence creates the bond.

Companions move toward one another to take care of needs—usually mutual needs. This emphasizes the Parent. They may use the adult (which is the best route) or the Child as they pass their time ("Did you hear the one about . . ."), but the functional ego state is Parent.

Functionary

Characteristics:

Bond-external
Nonsexual
Semiinclusive
parent, Adult, child

Stanley Milgram used the term "familiar stranger."[9] The term seems appropriate for the functionary level of relationships. At this level people meet occasionally either socially or professionally. They may be on a committee together. The relationship is likely to be more Adult ego state than any other.

Acquaintance

Characteristics:

No bond
Nonsexual
Inclusive
parent, adult, child

There is no bonding at the acquaintance level: People are like "ships passing in the night." Anyone can be an acquaintance, so the relationship is inclusive. There is probably little ego-state preference.

Spectrum of Relationships

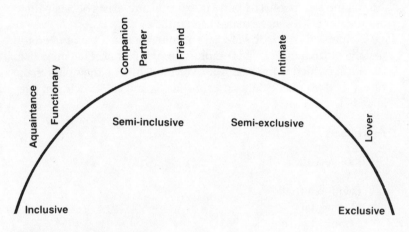

Changing Relationships

We can change in the relationships we have with others. Acquaintances can become Friends and Friends can become Intimates. An Acquaintance may become a Friend, then an Intimate, and finally our Lover. Relationships can regress. Why else are there divorces? Friends we had in school years later are no more than Acquaintances.

Confusion in Relationships

Changing or simultaneous relationships may create confusion. An Acquaintance may suddenly be treated as a Friend (or vice versa) and experience confusion and perhaps anger or fear. Paul was Mary's supervisor. Paul and his wife had been Intimates for several years with Mary and her husband. After Paul made an annual evaluation which was negative about Mary's work, they experienced confusion. Mary quit her job. The relationship went to Acquaintance. A person may experience confusion being appointed to a committee by a Friend or Intimate and ask, "Am I being appointed because of the contribution I can make or because I am a Friend?" When they have differing opinions on the committee, they may feel the friendship has been betrayed. "How can a Friend say that about my ideas?"

Sex outside the Lover relationship creates confusion. Sex does not create a Lover relationship. In fact, Thomas Oden says, "Sex may be alienating to intimacy as well as enabling it. Sex without interpersonal intimacy is like a diploma without an education."[10] Sex with a Friend may not only destroy the relationship with one's Lover but also with the Friend.

Living with Multiple Levels of Relationships

Each person lives with multiple levels of relations: Lover, Intimate, Friends, and so forth. Living only with Acquaintances, life is shallow. If one isolates at the Lover level only, one is ingrown. We need to accept the reality that we (and our mate) need all the levels of relationships. Learning and naming the levels of our relationships will help us understand how our needs are being met and keep integrity in those relationships.

This chapter has set out the levels of relationships and proposed the desirability of relating at the various levels. As we work with people, it is important to monitor our relationships. Teams are not machines set in place but people with relationships—hopefully growing, not eroding. Good team members need to care for one another—relationships—not just the task.

Notes

1. Alan McGinniss, *The Friendship Factor* (Minneapolis: Augsburg Press, 1979), pp. 29, 192.

2. Sidney Jourard, *The Transparent Self* (New York: Van Nostrand, Reinhold Co., 1964), p. 14.

3. Joseph Luft, *Group Process: An Introduction to Group Dynamics* (Palo Alto, Calif.: Mayfield Pub., 1970), p. 11.

4. Robert Dale, *Growing a Loving Church* (Nashville: Convention Press, 1974), p. 31.

5. Muriel James and Dorothy Jongeward, *Born to Win* (Reading, Mass.: Addison-Wesley, 1975), p.17.

6. Ibid., p. 18.

7. Ibid.

8. Howard J. Clinebell Jr., and Charlotte H. Clinebell, *The Intimate Marriage* (New York: Harper & Row, 1970).

9. C. Tavis, "The Frozen World of the Familiar Stranger: A conversation with Stanley Milgram," *Psychology Today,* 8 (1974), pp. 70-80.

10. Thomas Oden, *Game Free* (New York: Harper & Row), p. 33.

4
Clues About How You Relate

You probably don't see yourself as God sees you. Benhadad, the King of Syria, was ill and sent his servant, Hazael, to inquire of Elisha whether he would recover. Elisha replied that the King would recover but die. Elisha began to weep and Hazael asked why he was weeping. Elisha answered Hazael: "Because I know the evil that thou wilt do unto the children of Israel; their strong holds wilt thou set on fire, and their young men wilt thou slay with the sword, and wilt dash their children, and rip up their women with child." Shocked, Hazael answered, "Is thy servant a dog, that he should do this great thing?" Elisha answered, "The Lord hath shewed me that thou shalt be king over Syria" (2 Kings 8:12-13, KJV).

The point of the story is that God knows us better than we know ourselves. Hazael denied the possibility of the violence and treachery of acting like a mad dog, but two verses later there is the story of Hazael putting a wet cloth over the face of the weakened king so that he suffocated. God knows us, our revealed side and our shadow side. We need an Elisha to help us see the shadow side that God sees.

We don't see ourselves as others see us. I attended a seminar where one of the exercises was to mill around on a stage and experience the others in silence. We were given crayons of greasepaint to decorate each other's faces. I had never been in this institution, did not know the participants, and had never done this kind of exercise before. While I "played it cool," I was tense. One young woman asked if she could write on my face. Afterward, I noticed that people looked at my forehead where she had written and broke into a smile. After the exercise, they let us look into mirrors. She had written "SMILE" on my forehead. I

couldn't see what was written on my face and didn't know why
people smiled. How often we don't know what people see in us
to cause them to react to us as they do.

This summer I was visiting a professor where I had taught two
summers ago. One student in my class two years ago attended
summer school again this year. As two years ago, we shared
some of our life's crises and reflected on our future pilgrimages.
Toward the end of this summer I asked if she saw any changes in
me. She shot a sudden look at me and, as only a soul friend can
do, said, "Yes, you seem more sad." This was new information for
me. She saw something of my shadow side which was hidden
from me.

Our Many Selves

Elizabeth O'Connor wrote the book *Our Many Selves*.[1] She calls
attention to the "many" within each one of us. One morning I get
up and feel like one person and the next morning another. One
moment I feel like a king, the next moment a serf. I conquer like a
general before being intimidated like a child. I am a generous,
gracious giver who also acts like Scrooge. I am a loving and ten-
derhearted person who acts selfishly and insensitively. I am an
upright person who has monstrous thoughts, feelings, desires,
and lusts. This is not a problem of mental illness such as schizo-
phrenia. It is part of developing wholeness and identity as we
mature. Life is much like a new ship which is taken out on a
"shakedown" cruise in order to get the ship and crew in synchro-
nization.

If "our many selves" create problems for us, think what they do
for those to whom we relate. A person tries to relate to the one he
saw yesterday or to the mood or feeling she experienced in us at
our last meeting. Yesterday's self might have been kind, gentle,
and assured and today's self sarcastic and defensive. How can I
get a handle on this? There are several "selves" which may help
clarify "our many selves."

The Idealized Self

Each of us has an internalized picture of who we are or whom
we are destined to be. These usually begin to form in our early

childhood. Recently a friend said to me that when his grandson was born, the other set of grandparents bought him a hat with a hog ("hawg") on it which was a symbol of their alma mater. That sent my friend looking for a bison, the symbol of his alma mater. He said that there is nothing as vicious as the battle for the mind of a grandson. We may grow up thinking of ourselves as a "Yankee" or "Rebel"; privileged or servile; free or duty-bound.

One of the earliest questions a child faces in American society is "What do you want to be when you grow up?" In television Westerns we were introduced to ne'er-do-wells whose fathers had told them that they were "born for hangin'"—a destiny that they fulfilled. Have you seen people with the tattoo inscription "born loser"? I made a pastoral visit to a family whose mother put down the children's questions to me with such responses as: "Who do you think you are, asking Brother McCarty questions?" Those children have experienced prison, children out of wedlock, and serial marriages. The "idealized self" may not be the ideal person but is the image of self one has internalized.

The "idealized self" may be improperly founded. The romantic American notion that you can be anything you want may hinder developing an "ideal self" because it is diffuse rather than defined. Anyway, most of us can't be "anything we want." I may not be intellectually capable of being an Einstein or physically coordinated enough to become a sports superstar.

Vocation is only part of our "idealized self." Perhaps even more important is my image of self-worth. Our "idealized self" may be improperly formed, causing conceit. Paul admonished "not to think of himself more highly than he ought to think" (Rom. 12:3, KJV). My observation is that more people suffer from low self-esteem. They often have trouble accepting compliments and affirmation or have to receive profuse reassurance. After all, we are made in the image of God and the psalmist, speaking of humans, wrote:

> Yet thou hast made him little less
>   than God,
> and dost crown him with glory and
>   honor (Ps. 8:5).

Our environment may suppress our acting directly according to our idealized self. However, when we get involved in an activity, our idealized self eventually affects how we function unless we are aware of our idealized self and find ways to make it work for us instead of against us.[2]

The Functional Self

We take on roles in life. We become a student, husband or wife, father or mother, professor, pastor, citizen, or friend. The functional self is shaped by the expectations of others or society. Certain roles are expected to be fulfilled by sons and others by daughters. While challenged by the feminist movement, society has different role expectations for men and women.

The functional self may cause conflicts, even serious ones. The business executive is expected to be hard-nosed and profit oriented where money is the bottom line. In the role of deacon of the church, the businessman-deacon is expected to be sacrificial, caring, sensitive, and giving.

In the laboratory the scientist has the role of the cool, impartial, factual experimenter. As a representative of the church, the scientist is expected to be warm and convinced by faith of the truth which is nondemonstrable.

The Feeling Self

Humans are emotional creatures. Our feelings bring warmth and meaning to life and relationships. Our feelings often do not follow common logic but have reasons all their own. After all, "The heart has its reasons which reason knows nothing of." I may know that I am prepared for an exam, but my feelings of inadequacy create anxiety which cause mental blocks when I sit down to take the exam.

Feelings are not always in tune with reality. We may feel some people are angry with us because of disagreements in a committee meeting only to find that they aren't. We may feel that some believe that they are better than we are because they graduated from a particular school and find out they respect us.

The first time in my adult life that I had extended contact with any Roman Catholics was when I attended a training institute in Boston. Because of my family and church upbringing, my feelings about Roman Catholics were that their religion was one of convenience, that their prayers were mechanical and perfunctory, and that they had disdain for non-Catholics. While I attended the institute, our family physician discovered that our oldest daughter had a tumor on her arm. I shared my anxiety about my daughter with the group at the institute. I was overwhelmed by the concerned response, especially by the Roman Catholics. During group prayer, they prayed for her. Some of the sisters asked each day if I had heard any news and promised to pray for her during mass. I never had more deep concern expressed to me in my life. My feeling self did not match the reality.

The feeling self relates to our self-esteem and sense of competency. Self-esteem is a major human problem. I have seen competent persons who have achieved high positions unable to affirm themselves because of their impoverished background which eroded their self-esteem. A person who achieves may not feel it. Recently I had a conversation with a woman executive with whom I have been close for more than a decade. She has achieved. Her firm has given her raise after raise and more and more responsibility. However, there were signs of problems. She felt empty and unchallenged. In our conversation it came out. Although she is a gifted woman and has paid the price for her achievement, she never went to college. Everyone she supervises has a college education. Her self-worth suffered. She couldn't accept that she had learned from years of excellent experience what others learned in school. Her feeling self-esteem was not in touch with reality.

The Cultural Self

While I have for years believed in the power of culture over our lives, I have never seen it so vividly as I have since I have been teaching at Golden Gate Baptist Theological Seminary, where we have a large number of students from diverse ethnic origins. Many of these have become American citizens but they are still a part of their own cultural heritage. I have seen students who are

obviously a part of the Christian faith revert to the cultural mores
of animism when faced with certain issues. I have seen churches
organize reflecting the patterns of their cultural heritage.

The cultural self is an issue with all of us. I have seen the culture shock students undergo who come to San Francisco from the
South. Students who grow up in the West may have difficulty
understanding the attitude of students from the "Old South." De-
nominational officials tell the stories of what has happened to
Texas preachers who go to churches in the North.

The apostle Paul warned us not to be "moulded to this world"
(Rom. 12:2, Moffatt), but that cannot mean that we have no cultural self. Paul introduced himself as "a Jew" (Acts 21:39; 22:3).
He even called himself "a Pharisee, the son of a Pharisee" (Acts
23:6, KJV). We never step outside our cultural self, but we may
become more open and transcend our cultural self at times. I am
amused and disturbed at times when I find myself humming or
singing songs I learned in my childhood which reflect my childhood culture. Now I cringe at some of their crude expressions and
inappropriate theology, but they also touch a part of me as do few
other songs. My cultural self is there.

Culture is the way we structure and express our beliefs, ideas,
behavior, and relationships. Culture can become a prison (this is
what I believe Paul was warning against in Rom. 12:2). While we
can never become noncultural, we can be open to expand our
appreciation of other cultural forms. Our relationships will suffer
if we fail to note and appreciate the cultural selves of others.

The Community Self

We live in several communities: family, church, work, school,
and neighborhood. Ask a person who he or she is and the answer
may be "I'm a Jones" or "I'm a plumber" or "I'm a Texan." Much
of our identity comes from our community self. When our actual
community situation changes, our community self may struggle
to make the change. I have met people who told me they were
Missourians even though they haven't lived there for forty years.
I have a friend who moved from Dallas to Atlanta and it took him
four years to change from being a Dallas Cowboy fan to an Atlanta Falcon fan. He moved from Atlanta two years ago but still

talks about "our Falcons." A married couple establishes their own community and often experiences the conflict of their former "community selves."

We see the power of the community self in the present-day cults. The expectations of the community override any other "self." This phenomenon has been called mind control and brainwashing. Other "selves" may be diminished. The commune may demand to be the "family" and exact the devotion one once had to the natural family, thus changing the community self. A Zen Buddhist convert experiences a change in his or her cultural self. The guilt, fear, and hatred instilled into a person by a cult changes a person's feeling self. The Jonestown tragedy shows what can happen when people lose their many selves to one programmed self.

The Perceived Self

How do people see you? Regardless of the macho answer "I don't care what people think," how people perceive us is important. We tend to become how people perceive us—or react against it. The depth of our relationship with people is connected to how they perceive us. Seeing only our functional self won't lead to intimacy.

We may be confused by the different ways people perceive us. They often perceive us differently because they connect with our different selves. Some connect with our functional self, others our feeling self or community self. Recently I was going through the cafeteria line where I was a visiting professor and one of my students told me how much she appreciated my warmth, gentleness, and sensitivity. When I sat down to eat lunch, a professor chuckled and told me that he had met a former student of mine who said that I was the meanest professor he had ever had. I want to accept the first evaluation and pass the second off as a student's humor about a former professor. Probably they were both responding to my "many selves."

Our many selves can be the source of problems for us if we are unable to hold these as paradoxes of our lives. We need to accept the fact of our many selves and their paradoxes, yet be in control enough that we do not feel torn apart by them. When we say with the poet, "To thine own self be true," we must be able to ask, "Which self?" We need to keep the paradox from becoming so disparate that we cannot be whole and healthy. A Christian who is obsessed to break all the Commandments repeatedly has lost the paradox to compulsion and wholeness to partitioned behavior.

It is also dangerous to try to solve the paradox by trying to have only one self. The result can be legalism, racism, fanaticism, or egotism. Wholism is not being one "self" but the integration of the paradoxical "selves."

Relating Differently to Different People

How do I want to relate to someone? I may only want to relate to George in the next office through my functional self, my role. When I talk to George, we are two accountants, professors, or plumbers. While the functional self is an appropriate way to relate, if this is the only self a person feeds, it will lead to onesidedness and hollowness deteriorating the power of the other important selves.

Relating depends on being able to identify the "self" from which the other person relates and being enough in control of our many selves to respond appropriately. We may not understand why a person is not more aggressive to take a public stand on a moral issue or do door-to-door visitation. Their cultural self inhibits them from copying your extravertive and individualistic approach. Their cultural self may make it important for them to operate in a more oblique way and make their visitation one family visiting another family.

A woman grew up with strong inhibitions about showing feelings in public. She fell in love with a young man who was demonstrative of his feelings in public. The conflict nearly destroyed the relationship. Their feeling selves connected in private but not in public.

Know Thyself

According to tradition, Socrates' primary rule for wisdom was "know thyself." If we enrich our working with people, we will need to know ourselves to relate well to others. We may not need to know much about ourselves to relate to some people, but the "many selves" of others do not match "our many selves" and require self-knowledge.

One of the parts of self-knowledge is the paradox in our lives. While I have referred to an individual's paradox earlier, Thomas Oden carries paradox further.

The paradoxical structure of personhood may be seen from the following two-column delineation. Personhood, and thus interpersonal meeting, is both:

Nature	Spirit
Enmeshed in causality	Capable of self-direction
Necessity	Freedom
Limited by natural factors	Capable of self-transcendence
Body	Soul
Existence in time	Present to the eternal
Finite	Infinite
Animal	Rational
Passion	Imagination
Instinct	Cultural creation

In interpersonal meeting, persons confront the paradox that they live both as children of nature and yet they transcend nature through spirit.[3] Later Oden sums up paradox as a problem in relationships: "All is this essentially contradictory nature of personhood that cunningly and sometimes tragically comes into play in personal transactions and confounds every oversimplified description of a given interaction."[4]

Knowing ourselves will mean getting in touch with the shadow side of our selves. There is that dark side deep within each of us. It is made up of confusion, compulsions, guilt, fears, and obsessions we may never have admitted to our conscious level or may suppress each time one of those dragons raises its head. Or we may allow it to live only in our fantasies but never reveal it to anyone (unless it is to our therapist). But the shadow side is there. Every light upon an object casts a shadow. Conversely every shadow means that there is light.

Looking Through Spectacles to Find Clues

Let me put two analogies together. Immanuel Kant suggested that we look at all reality through two pairs of spectacles. I suggest that we have many pairs of spectacles through which we may look at life, particularly relationships. One pair may help us understand one relation and a second pair another and on and on. Obviously the trick is to get the right pair of spectacles for each relationship. In fact, it may take several pairs to understand each relationship. Spectacles really distort the vision of reality so we can see more clearly. So we should recognize when we use "spectacles" to look at relationships that some distortion is taking place but that it is the price of seeing clearly.

The second analogy is that of clues. I may know the result but I don't know how it happened. I need clues to understand it. Another way of talking about clues is to have facts but not to know what they mean. I need a clue which will be the key to unlock the mystery.

The double analogy is that the spectacles will help me "see" what is going on and provide me with the clue to decipher the meaning of a relationship. We have picked up some spectacles and clues in life. I might say, "I know he was lying because he wouldn't look me in the eye." Or I might say, "I don't know why, I just had this feeling that he wasn't telling the truth." In the first statement I know what the spectacle is: direct eye contact. In the second the spectacle remains a part of my nonconscious experience, but it is real.

Every person and relationship is different and unique, but there are patterns in relationships. Even when we experience the bizarre, there is a pattern of irrationality. Our job is not to destroy the uniqueness of a person or the individuality of a relationship but to find the pattern or patterns of relationships. Every person is different but there are brunettes, blonds, and redheads. Recognizing that a person is blond does not destroy his or her uniqueness; it only identifies and distinguishes a pattern of hair color. Spectacles and clues are not boxes to lock people in and destroy their uniqueness but a way to find a pattern which will help us understand them—and their uniqueness.

One reason we need spectacles and clues is that most of us have patterned responses in life. You have seen a person marry a "loser," divorce and marry another "loser." Others come to depend on us because we do have patterns. We may say, "I know he'll blow up" or "He'll forgive" or "He will give up." Spectacles and clues provide categories that explain what a person will do. Spectacles and clues provide categories by which we can anticipate and respond to others.

There are some images which help us. As I said about the spectacles, there may be some distortion but they are helpful. After all, distortions serve us. We can speak of an object being round, but at earth's gravity, nothing is perfectly round. We live with the distortion, but the notion of roundness helps us visualize an object.

Three Ego States

Transactional Analysis provides several spectacles to help us examine relationships. One is the distinction of the three ego states: parent, adult, and child. These have nothing to do with age or our family status. They do clarify how we handle information, people, and relationships.

The parent ego state is characterized by oughtness. A person in a parent ego state may be nurturing parent or critical parent. The nurturing parent expresses oughtness by taking care of someone or some situation. This person ought to care and does, perhaps even trying to rescue someone who doesn't need or want to be rescued.

The critical parent expresses oughtness by being judgmental and giving prohibitions and is often legalistic. This person has a strong and usually external standard of right and wrong and makes value judgments for others.

The parent ego state is the composite of "messages" we have received, especially as children. We were given rules and mottoes we internalized and later call on to guide our behavior and evaluate others.

The adult ego state gathers information and determines probabilities on the basis of logic. The adult ego state deals with factual statements rather than value statements.

The child ego state is the feeling part. Play, fantasy, enjoyment, and fun are likely to come from the child. The child may be adaptive, rebellious, natural, or a little professor.

The adaptive child wants to please and say yes.

The rebellious child wants to say no. Persons in this ego state react negatively, especially to someone relating to them from the critical parent ego state. A youngster may be generally adaptive until adolescence and then begin to act out of the rebellious child ego state. However, a person may change back and forth from hour to hour or person to person.

The natural child is the fun child who lets down inhibitions, enjoys, and is the comic who can make you laugh. Playing games and fantasies come when we are in our natural child.

The "little professors" like one-up-manship. They like to tell you the inside story. They may be sarcastic and elitist.[5]

All of these ego states (and substates) are important for healthy people and relationships. We need to help others (nurturing parent). Each needs a sense of right and wrong and the ability to analyze situations by our values (critical parent). We need facts and logic (adult). Society is based on adaptiveness and families on pleasing others (adaptive child). Without the ability to resent and say no, we will never be our own person (rebellious child). "Showing off" is one of the ways we experiment in life (little professor). Problems arise when I spend too much time in one ego state.

The Ego Gram

The ego gram has been developed to find out how much we act out of each of these.

Fill out an ego gram by shading the percentage of time you spend in each ego state. All the ego states combined should add up to 100 percent. Have others fill them out on you as they perceive you. In the example you will notice the person is overly invested in the critical parent and deals mostly with values, not facts (adult). There is not much genuine, internal emotion (child).

The ego states provide a pair of spectacles by which we can gather clues about the relationship. You will work with a critical parent differently than a natural child. The critical parent may be

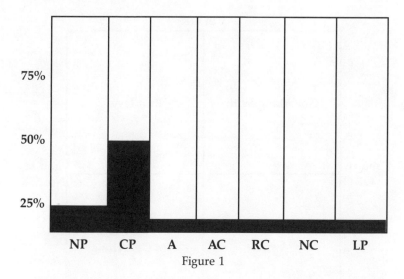

Figure 1

driven by what he "ought to do," while the natural child turns everything into a party.

I may intend to relate to a person adult to adult. He may tend to relate to people out of his rebellious child. Our relationship (transaction) will be in difficulty unless I am conscious of what is going on and find an appropriate way to respond. The effective working relationship depends on my ability to do this.

The OK Corral

There is another pair of spectacles which may be helpful that developed from TA. It is the "OK Corral" based on the theme of "I'm OK, You're OK." Examine Figure 2 on the following page to see its components.

The quadrants show the relationships which can be expected with the various attitudes toward self and others. In the upper left quadrant the person operates from an "I'm OK—You're OK" stance, and the result is that a good relationship is possible. He or she can get along with others.

The upper right quadrant shows the position of "I'm OK—You're Not OK." A person in this stance will try to take advantage

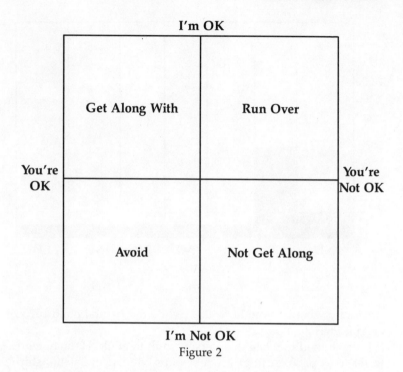

I'm OK

Get Along With	Run Over
Avoid	Not Get Along

You're OK

You're Not OK

I'm Not OK
Figure 2

of others—run over them. After all, they are not OK, so what difference does it make. They don't count. They are nobodies.

The lower left quadrant represents the "You're OK—I'm Not OK" position. The person in this position will try to avoid and flee since he is overwhelmed or intimidated by the other person. This person will fear being used. This position makes good relationships difficult.

The fourth position is the "I'm Not OK—You're Not OK" position. Building relationships on this position is like trying to build a skyscraper on quicksand. It won't stand for long.

The Faith Corral

The "Faith Corral" uses the format of the "OK Corral" to picture relationships with God. I have a hunch that the "OK Corral"

Figure 3

and the "Faith Corral" are related. The relationship we have with God is mirrored with people.

Persons who feel that they are OK and God is OK are the persons of faith. Faith, as used here, is not doctrine but the New Testament sense of faith, which is trust. Faith is a personal relationship. Experiencing God's sense of worth and the human reflective worth provides the framework for a faith relationship.

Persons who operate from an "I'm OK—God's Not OK" stance have a religion of magic. My first reaction is "Who would say that 'God is not OK?'" Of course, few people who confess there is a God would verbalize this, but unconsciously they operate this way. They make God an "errand boy." Prayer becomes our "orders of the day" for God. As in animism, this person seeks to manipulate the strange power of God. This is a defective relationship rather than one of faith. The relationship is not a faith relationship but an extractive relationship: God, save me, heal me, make me rich, give me victory, don't let them die, etc.

The position that "God's OK—I'm not OK" is one of doubt. Notice that doubt is not God's problem but a human problem. Doubt erodes the ability to have a faith relationship.

Cynicism is the result of a position of "God's not OK" and "I'm Not OK." The cynic has a shadow view of things. Relation with God is least possible here. The cynic can only respond with "black humor," not faith.

I would not suggest that any of us have faith so complete that we do not experience the other quadrants. Hopefully, our faith is growing. Perhaps the Johari Window is not only a key to human relationships but our relationship with God. As we are able to be open and vulnerable and accept feedback, we can grow in our faith relationship. We may even expect this movement in the Christian life. The patterns seen in a growing Christian might appear like the sequences following.

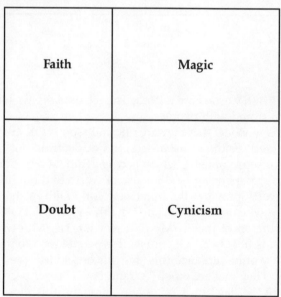

Figure 4

Faith
Magic
Doubt
Cynicism
Figure 5

Faith
Magic
Doubt
Cynicism
Figure 6

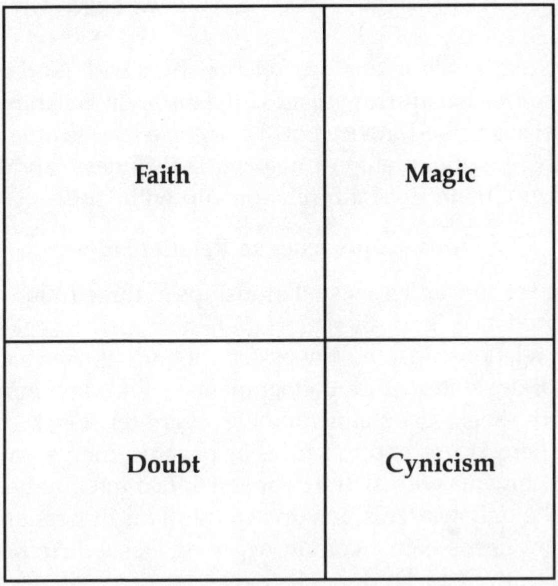

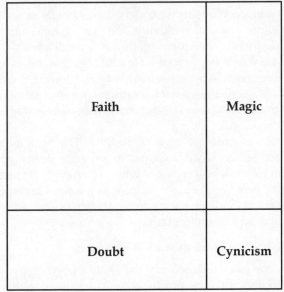

Again, my hunch is that our relationships with God and people are somewhat mirror images. If you want to know how a person relates to God, notice how he or she relates to other people. Where there is the quality of respect, faithfulness, and trust toward others, there is a faith relationship with God.

Three Approaches to Relationships

One set of spectacles sees relationships in three frames: attachment, avoidance, and alienation. When a person seeks attachment in relationships, he hopes for a bonding, mutuality, and emotional ties. Life without attachments is grim and empty. The person who seeks deep attachment in every relationship is unrealistic. There is not enough time or psychic energy to develop deep attachments with all the people we encounter in the modern world. The only way this person can fulfill his or her compulsive attachment needs is in a commune, in an isolated Arctic village, or on a South Sea island.

Avoidance is meeting with people but not bonding with them. The person who only uses avoidance relationships depends on externals and, relationshipwise, is hollow. Avoidance is intimacy avoidance, not physical avoidance. We may "bounce off" people all the time without developing intimacy. I recall a Southern gentleman who was always proper. He said the right things and was the gracious host. Anyone sensitive to relationships could tell that you always met a mask of propriety, but the real person behind the mask withdrew. His outward graciousness was a way to cover his avoidance.

Alienation is usually a sign of hostility. The hostility may be internalized rather than a response to a specific person or event. Alienation may not be a signal of when a person "gets mad" but, rather, may be a life position out of which a person responds to people or events. Such persons do not simply flee (avoidance) but plant land mines as they retreat.

Instruments Which Help

During the twentieth century the field of psychology has matured, and one of the by-products has been many evaluative instruments. These are not magic, but are helpful tools to get data.

Good instruments are like mirrors; they show us our own image. Instruments do not create any characteristics; they are only short-cuts to self-knowledge and help eliminate our tendency to put ourselves down or value ourselves more highly than we ought.

Psychologists design instruments to measure a variety of things. Some design instruments to measure psychological traits, especially personality problems.[7] The Taylor-Johnson Temperament Analysis is a "method of measuring a number of important and comparatively independent personality variables or behavioral tendencies which influence personal, social, marital, parental, family, scholastic, and vocational adjustment."[8] The Taylor-Johnson Temperament Analysis measures nine traits and their opposites: nervous (composed); depressive (lighthearted); active-social (quiet); expressive-responsive (inhibited); sympathetic (indifferent); subjective (objective); dominant (submissive); hostile (tolerant); and self-disciplined (impulsive).

The Taylor-Johnson is a helpful pair of spectacles for relationships. It is most helpful when two people or a team can take the Taylor-Johnson and review the results for implications in relationships. When two people take it, they can project how they perceive the other person.

The Firo-B Inventory examines how people behave in relationships. It measures how much they want or avoid social interaction, how much control they want to exercise or how much structure they need and the need for intimacy and affection.[9]

The Myers-Briggs Type Indicator is an instrument based on Jungian psychology. It describes sixteen types of personality. There are four basic categories which form the inventory: extrovert-introvert; sensing-intuitive; thinking-feeling; and judging-perceiving. The inventory offers many clues as to how team members will relate to one another.[10]

Bi-Polar Psychology Seminar was developed by Dr. Jay Thomas. It provides clues as to the way persons function in relationships and vocational situations. There are eight basic categories with the recognition that people use all categories but have one in which they are most at home.[11]

Teleometrics International of The Woodlands, Texas, has developed several instruments especially for the business sector, but they are helpful to give clues to individuals and staffs of all organizations. The Personal Relations Survey uses the format of the Johari Window to determine how a person relates to supervisors, colleagues, and employees.

The Styles of Leadership Survey by Jay Hall and Martha Williams is also a Teleometric instrument. It provides information about a person's leadership style based on five different styles. The styles relate to the strength of the person's concern for people and concern for purpose (tasks).[12]

No one instrument will be as helpful as multiple instruments. The more instruments taken, the more they correct one another and provide views of our personalities from varying perspectives. The many pairs of spectacles give us the clues to look for as we examine the mystery of human relationships.

Notes

1. Elizabeth O'Connor, *Our Many Selves* (New York: Harper & Row), p. 201.

2. Transactional Analysis has helped to clarify some aspects of the idealized self by discussions of "life scripts." For more information see Claude Steiner's book, *Scripts People Live* (New York: Grove Press, 1974).

3. Thomas Oden, *Game Free*, p. 121.

4. Ibid.

5. For a full treatment of the ego states see Thomas Harris, *I'm OK—You're OK* (New York: Avon Books, 1973), p. 317.

6. Muriel James and Dorothy Jongeward, *Born to Win* (Reading, Mass.: Addison-Wesley, 1975), p. 299.

7. The MMPI (Minnesota Multiphasic Personality Inventory) and the Rorschach Test are such instruments

8. *Taylor-Johnson Temperament Analysis Manual*, 1980 Revision, p. 1, Psychological Publications, Los Angeles, p. 59.

9. Firo-B stands for Fundamental Interpersonal Relations Inventory-Behavior and is published by Consulting Psychology Press, 527 College Ave., Palo Alto, Calif., 94306. It was developed by Dr. William Schutz.

10. Myers Briggs Type Indicator.

11. Bi-Polar Psychology.

12. Teleometrics information may be obtained from Teleometrics, 1755 Woodstead Court, The Woodlands, Texas, 77380.

5
A Supporting Cast

Several years ago I was commissioned to write case studies on four Baptist associations which had unusually good records in starting new churches. When I had finished the research, one issue stood out. Three of the four associations had provided support systems for the mission pastors. Having three out of four associations with purposely developed support groups is highly unusual. They must play an important role in the associations' success in starting new churches.

Superstars don't make it on their own; they need a supporting cast. The greatest actor or actress needs the supporting cast, including script writers and prop managers. The greatest pitcher needs a good team behind him to win. The support system is incomplete if it only cares for the tasks. There needs to be affirmation and emotional support. A supporting cast needs to provide affirmation, opportunity for growth, and relief from boredom. There may need to be the support of a mentor, but individual support is not enough; support demands a team. Nowhere is this more true than in the ministry.

Barnabas

Barnabas was the model of a support person. He served as a mentor to Paul. When Paul was not allowed to join the disciples after his conversion, "Barnabas came to his help" (Acts 9:27, GNB). Later Barnabas went to Tarsus to find the depressed Paul and brought him to Antioch where a support group rallied around Paul (Acts 11:22ff.) It was from Antioch that Paul and Barnabas were sent out on their missionary journey through Asia Minor (Acts 13:1-3). Barnabas' name means "son of consolation," an encourager. Wherever Paul and Barnabas went, they took the

message of encouragement, strengthening the Christians and
churches (see Acts 13:15,43; 14:23). I wonder what would have
happened had the encourager, Barnabas, not found the despair-
ing Paul in Tarsus and encouraged him.

The Mentor

A staff, paid or volunteer, needs a mentor and a support system. These will enrich the staff, bring meaning and growth, and
assist them in their work. Without support a staff will not reach
its potential as a group; nor will the individuals develop their full
capabilities as leaders.

Executives find this to be true in business. Harry Levinson
wrote:

> A major factor in a manager's development is the opportunity
> for him to identify with those who have more experience, skill, and
> power than he has.
>
> The coaching and appraisal process, as usually carried out in U.S.
> business, falls short of the mark because it does not support strong
> relationships and contacts between a boss and his subordinate.
>
> Among the most important reasons for this failure are that most
> line executives do not give enough time and thought to working
> with their juniors; the climate in business is not tolerant enough of
> mistakes and individual needs to learn; and rivalry between
> bosses and subordinates tends to be repressed instead of acknowl-
> edged.[1]

Another article in the same publication is entitled "Everyone
Who Makes It Has a Mentor."[2]

The Support Group

The leader is not only a primary actor but the mentor to others
and the enabler of a support group. The leader needs to be the
Barnabas and provide encouragement—both professionally *and*
personally. The leader is more than an organizational head; he or
she is the encourager of persons. Each of these persons has
dreams, difficulties, fears, anxieties, and feelings. A good leader
does not run past these and give attention only to tasks. Taking
care of the needs of the persons on a staff is the primary role of a

leader. Support is not optional for a good leader; it is the leader's first responsibility.

My definition of supervision begins: "Supervision is the development of a support system."[3] I understand ministry is to support people, not to tear them down. Ministry provides the support so that people can grow in grace and knowledge and fulfill what God has for them to do.

Everyone needs support. Education does not eliminate the need for support. Bill Pinson, executive director of the Baptist General Convention of Texas, wrote: "I have discovered many people need encouragement. Appearances are misleading. Successful business persons, professionals, politicians, actors, artists, teachers, students, farmers, and many others share a sense of discouragement with others."[4] A professional church staff is not exempt from the need of support. They may be trained and professional, but they are human.

Affirmation

Affirmation is the crucial part of support. Many times people have confessed to me that they didn't get affirmation from their leader. When someone has told me that they received great affirmation from their leader, I have seen a special reverence for their leader in their eyes and expressive voice. Affirmation is a key to Christian growth and service. Thomas Kain in his book *The Healing Touch of Affirmation* says, "The word affirmation comes from the Latin *affirmare* and means to make firm, to give strength, to make strong."[5] These are the things we want to do for those who work with us.

Affirmation does not come easily for some of us. We are much better at criticizing. Only the secure person can easily affirm others. We are taught many things in school—how to parse verbs, the dates of history, and mathematical formulas. Who has had a course in how to affirm? No one consciously teaches us to affirm others. How can we learn this important skill? Thomas Kain wrote:

> Ways of affirmation differ, but all are important. Affirmation can
> be visual, e.g. a responsive smile; tactile, e.g. an embrace; audi-

tory, e.g. an expression of sympathy; and it can be spiritual, e.g. a shared prayer.[6]

We have in our possession the power to bless others. We need to realize we have that power and use it. How many staff persons (as well as spouses and children) are passionately hungry for an affirming word of blessing? I shared with a doctoral candidate the reports of how his sarcasm and critical attitude were hurting his ministry. He knew it and asked what to do about it. I suggested that he discipline himself to affirm three people each day purposefully and consciously. Several months later he told me how difficult that had been but added that it had changed his life, his ministry, and his marriage. He had experienced the power of blessing.

Growing People

The leader supports by helping people grow. The leader does not only administer programs but also is a catalyst for growth among those on the team. For growth to occur, the leader may need to provide learning opportunities. These may be informal or one-to-one sessions where the leader takes time to share ideas, demonstrate skills, lend literature or help in an experiment. The personal involvement and caring of the leader will be acts of support.

Growth is not optional; it is a part of support. We should not be so concerned about the growth of people in the congregation that we overlook the growth needs of the staff. I feel I am a failure as the leader of a person who works with me and does not outgrow the job in three years. I don't infer that a person has to change institutions every three years because most jobs can be upgraded through enrichment. The leader who supports and helps a staff member grow always risks losing the staff member to a more challenging situation. But think of the alternative. A person who does not grow feels "I'm not OK" and usually compensates by being critical. That is not a good working environment for the rest of the staff and will create negativism in the whole institution. The person who does not grow will try to make things safe by resisting any serious expansion.

Support and Staff Turnover

Developing a support system for staff is important to combat staff turnover. While there are factors outside the institution which create reasons for people to leave, there are significant reasons within which help people stay. Vincent Flowers and Charles Hughes have done research on employee turnover and suggest that the reason employees stay is inertia. They point out two factors which affect inertia: "First, within the company, there is the issue of job satisfaction. Second, there is the 'company environment' and the degree of comfort an individual feels within it."[7] A good support system reinforces the sense of the persons' own worth and achievements. It helps the staff know where they stand, who they are, so they are comfortable in their situations.

I observed a staff who spent an inordinate amount of time consoling each other and wondering about their roles. They put a lot of time into looking for other jobs. There was no special problem—only the benign neglect of their supervisor to give them supportive attention and affirmation. The supervisor never threatened or berated them; he just stayed away, worked at other tasks, and left the staff to their tasks. As a result, he spent a large amount of time interviewing people for staff positions and trying to cover the holes left by departed staff. Had he developed a support system where he consciously met with the staff members to listen, help them, and affirm them, he would have taken less time than he did dealing with turnover problems.

Becoming a Team

Developing a support system means creating a team. This applies to volunteers as well as a paid staff. A collection of people is not necessarily a team. It takes special work and time to create a team. A team forms through interaction, time, goals, and mutuality. A team has a sense of interdependence and belongs to one another. Persons on a team know that they can turn to the other team members for information, help, and emotional support. Team members receive their affirmation from one another. The work of the team becomes more important than the tasks of an individual where there is a genuine team. Coaches in various sports know this. Affirmation comes from what the team achieves rather than from a single person's achievement.

Teams form following patterns of group dynamics. A leader does not announce that a collection of people is a team and they become a team. People have to want to be a team and work together to make it happen. Even if they want a team, they have to go through some rather well-defined stages to become a team. Experts on group dynamics have identified some of the stages. Although they differ, they have common elements in their presentations.

Charles Keating presents a theory of group development known as Cog's Ladder which has five steps. Keating says, "The first step is the *Polite* stage, a time of ritual when members feel a need to be liked; it is a time to become acquainted, to share some general interests and to handle first impressions.[8]

"The second step is the *The Why We're Here* stage, a time to try to define the purposes and goals of the group. Hidden agendas— that is, the individual reasons for belonging to the group and plans for using the group—as well as cliques are most likely to begin to surface in this stage."[9] This is a critical stage. Individuals need approval. They need to discuss the group's goals. While individual goals should be honored and as many included as possible, there will have to be some compromises for them to become a team.

The *Bid for Power* is the third stage.[10] Individuals and cliques try to influence the group. There is competition, and leadership is at stake. This stage can be mild if the leader is secure and knowledgeable about group formation. If there are compulsive neurotics in the group, it will likely be stormy. If the leader is threatened or does not realize that this is normal, it can be difficult. If the people in the group are very assertive, there may be a lot of energy spent in this stage and the outcome will depend on the leader guiding but not repressing the energy. The word *power* is often thought of negatively; however, people and groups must have some power or they can accomplish nothing. The issue is directing the power toward team goals and not abusing it.

The fourth step is the *Constructive* stage.[11] It is in this stage that the collection of individuals becomes a team. There are attitudinal changes. People listen to one another, are more open, and accept differences. Decisions and solutions can be reached in this stage, and real teamwork begins. Identity as a team builds.

Keating says, "The fifth step on the Ladder is the *Esprit* stage, in which the members feel high group morale and intense personal goals, they do not affect the group adversely and there is a bond of trust."[12]

Maxwell Pattison proposes developmental stages to which he give the interesting names of Storming, Forming, Norming, Performing.[13] It seems to me he has erroneously inverted Storming and Forming. The process should read: Forming, Storming, Norming, and Performing.

The first stage of a team has enthusiasm and idealism. The members are going to be great friends and accomplish great goals. There are groups that never get beyond this stage—they are all talk, celebrating fellowship which has never been tested for reality. Some groups start to move toward stage 2 (Storming) and retreat back to the euphoria of stage 1 as soon as someone speaks a harsh word. The leader needs to be aware that the euphoria won't last forever and be emotionally prepared to moved into stage 2—Stormy.

Since most people would like to avoid serious conflict, the Storming stage is difficult. Some people bail out disillusioned, fearful, frustrated, or angry. Others add fuel to the fire storm by organizing cliques, making guilt pronouncements, or participating in mutiny. The leader may react one of three ways. First the leader may turn to self-incrimination and ask, "Where did I go wrong?" The response others make is to blame and ask, "What is wrong with them?" The third possible response is to treat this stage as a necessary phase and bring the people through it with as few cuts and bruises as possible.

The Storm stage is necessary and should be helpful. Where there is a democratic rather than an autocratic process, people with different goals, values, life-styles, loyalties, and methods will need to negotiate a working relationship. There is no way to do this without conflict. The leader's job is to see that conflict finally brings people closer together rather than destroying one another.

The Forming stage is where the individuals begin to become a team. In this stage they clarify values, goals, and roles—which could not have happened without the Storming stage. Fear of differences begins to become respect for the variety of gifts. They begin to find common values beneath the variety of rhetoric.

Having gone through the first three stages it is possible to move into the performing stage. In this stage the team can get things done. Now they are a real team. They have set their common goals, determined their roles, and have developed their leadership.

Dangers in Team Building

Here are some observations about team development. They may seem disconcerting—especially to impatient, aggressive leaders. First, you can move too quickly through the stages. Pattison was correct in calling them developmental stages. Being in a hurry to "get the team on the field" is a temptation, but it is like picking fruit green which tastes a little sour and gives a giant stomachache later. People need time to internalize the stages. I know of no rule which tells us how long each stage will be. Different people, organizations, and situations create different time patterns. The stages are not so clear-cut that you can usually tell at any one meeting whether you have passed into another stage. You may see signs that you have reached a new stage only to see the group revert back at your next meeting. You often have people who are ready to move into the next stage before the whole group is ready. Also, the group may be ready before one individual is ready.

The temptation is to try to skip a stage. It may seem the group is ready to move from stage 1 to stage 3, but sometimes the group will revert to stage 2. There is great danger to the group in this situation. They will have invested extra time which is now lost. Since people felt some sense of being a team, they are more likely to become disillusioned and give up.

When we have worked through the stages with one group and

begin with a new group, we may try to take up with the new group where we left off with the former group. Every group has its own pilgrimage. Even where some have been in the former group, the new group has to become its own team. Ministers face this problem when they leave one church to go to another. They have to begin all over again. They have to earn their leadership again and go through the process to form a new team.

A group which has moved beyond stage 1 and has added a new member faces problems. The group has to go back to stage 1 and start over if they wish to add the new person to the team. Where only one person is added to a large team, this may not be as severe but often becomes business as usual. In that situation the newcomer feels like and remains an outsider.

A team which is given a new task has to recycle through the stages. This may be done more quickly because of information, trust, and relationships—but it needs to happen.

It is more important to remember that this is a *normal* process, not a diabolical scheme. You expect a child to go through infancy and cry; through adolescence and pout. Becoming a team is a developmental process in human relations. Each new group is trying to birth a new team.

The Team as a Support Group

The team is important not only to get a job done but to be a support group. The group that becomes a real team cares for and takes care of one another. Where people are put together only to do a job, they feel used. People who become part of a caring team—a support group—feel a sense of fulfillment. Fulfillment brings the job satisfaction Flowers and Hughes discussed. The feeling of being used brings dissatisfaction and ultimately mutiny.

Developing a support group is not only an issue where there is a professional staff but also where the staff is volunteer. People who serve as volunteers also need to feel a part of the team and need to find support. Every committee should be a team and support group.

Notes

1. Harry Levinson, "A Psychologist Looks at Executive Development" in *Paths Toward Personal Progress: Leaders Are Made Not Born* (Boston: Harvard Business Review, 1983), p. 56.

2. Eliza G. C. Collins and Patricia Scott, "Everyone Who Makes It Has a Mentor," pp. 135-147 (above book).

3. See Doran McCarty, *The Supervision of Ministry Students*, p. 8. Home Mission Board, Atlanta, 1978, pp. 157 and *The Supervision of Mission Personnel*, p. 21, Home Mission Board, Atlanta, 1983, p. 203.

4. William Pinson, Jr. *Ready to Minister* (Nashville: Broadman Press, 1984), pp. 100, 131.

5. Thomas Kane, *The Healing Touch of Affirmation* (Whitensville: Affirmation Books, 1976), p. 22.

6. Ibid., p. 24.

7. Vincent S. Flowers and Charles L. Hughes, "Why Employees Stay," p. 50, *Harvard Business Review*, July-August, 1973, Vol. 451, No. 4.

8. Charles J. Keating, *The Leadership Book* (Ramsey, N.J.: Paulist Press, 1982), pp. 30, 133.

9. Ibid., p. 31.

10. Ibid.

11. Ibid., p. 32.

12. Ibid.

13. E. Mansell Pattison, *Pastor and Parish—a Systems Approach* (Philadelphia: Fortress Press, 1977), pp. 58-62, 88.

6
Working with a Staff

Within the past two weeks representatives of two churches visited me with problems related to church staffs. The first visitor asked me to recommend a pastor who was good at working with a church staff. Their church recently lost their nationally known pastor, but his fame had not kept away staff problems. The second visitor asked if I would be a consultant to their church to help with their staff problems.

Staff problems are neither new nor unusual. Jesus even had a problem staff—the twelve. Simon Peter was so impetuous that his colleagues never knew what he would do or say next. James and John tried to put one over and gain leadership prominence. And, of course, there was Judas. Was it in exasperation that Jesus once said to them, "How long shall I put up with you?" (Mark 9:19, NASB).

Staff persons are leaders, and someone on the staff has the responsibility to be the leader of leaders. In a church it is nearly universal that the pastor is the leader of the leaders. If there is a paid staff, the pastor is their leader. If there is no paid staff, the pastor is still the leader. Volunteers in the church are the staff. The way the pastor leads depends on the pastor's style of leadership. There may be a variety of images to describe leadership styles. The description most helpful to me is "the leader provides." Where the pastor is autocratic, more of the providing depends on the pastor. If the pastor is more democratic and participative, the staff does more providing. Therefore what I have to say about providing is not necessarily only for the pastor. When the pastor shares the leadership with the staff members, they share being providers.

Autocratic   Participative

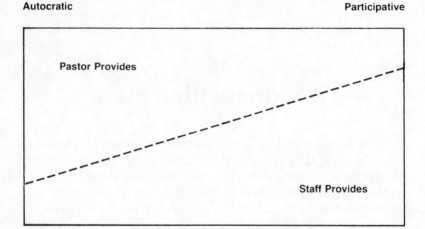

Figure 1

The autocratic leader maintains the weight of the work even with a staff. The participative leader bears the responsibility of leadership but distributes the pressure.

Provide Leadership

The first word I have for a minister who wants to be a leader is, "Do your job—minister!" I am not referring only to ministering to the congregation or the lost but ministering to the staff. The minister's innermost circle of responsibility is to the staff so they can minister to the congregation and the lost. I have heard the lament of associates who felt the pastor neglected their needs when the pastor would never neglect the needs of parishioners. I have heard the complaints of lay leaders that, since they were leaders, the pastor never visited and ministered to them.

The second word I have for a minister who wants to be a leader is, "Do your job—lead!" When a mechanic becomes a service manager in a garage, the temptation is to get back under the hood and fix a car. The service manager's new job is to coordinate, assign, and advise. The service manager must leave the old job for his new one. I asked about a minister who recently left the pastorate to become an executive director of a Baptist association. I was told that the new executive greatly missed the evangelistic visitation he did as a pastor. As admirable as evangelistic visitation is, the executive now has a new job of enabling others to do evangelism. The crucial question for leaders is whether they are doing *their* job or their *former* job. I accepted the task to be a consultant for a ministry where there was a fine, gifted minister. He had started the ministry, had seen it grow and slump several times. He had a special gift of one-to-one ministry; but when the ministry grew and there was a staff, he continued ministering the way he began. The growth meant that his job had changed, but he was still doing the old job, not the new one. If there was to be progress beyond a certain point, he would have to do *his* job—a new job in the same ministry.

Keith Davis provides a graph which shows the different roles of various leaders.[1]

The graph shows that various leaders have different jobs. A leader who has functioned at one level and moves to another has to change roles or become ineffective in the new role.

Styles of Leadership

Your job is to be a leader. There are different styles of leadership. Not everyone accepts the reality of different styles of leadership. I have a friend who is a strong-willed, hard-driving pastor. Once we had a conversation about a mutual friend who is a quiet, unassuming, and democratic type of leader. My strong-willed friend spoke negatively about our mutual friend and his lack of forcefulness. However, our mutual friend had gone to a troubled congregation, stayed ten years, and left it a healed and vigorous congregation. The congregation needed his style of leadership.

There have been many arguments over what the qualities of a leader are. Paul Hersey and Ken Blanchard wrote, "For many years the most common approach to the study of leadership concentrated on leadership traits per se, suggesting that there were certain characteristics, such as physical energy or friendliness, that were essential for effective leadership.[2] Hersey and Blanchard challenge this approach. They say, "Empirical studies suggest that leadership is a dynamic process, varying from situation to situation with changes in leaders, followers and situation."[3] There are four elements which are leadership variables: leader, followers, goals, and environment. Since these are different in each situation, leadership has to be different to be effective.

Putting it in perspective, there are different styles of leadership, and one style works with one group of people but other styles are needed with other situations. One style may work at the beginning but later another style may be needed. This is approximately what Hersey and Blanchard mean by "situational leadership."

The idea of multiple styles of leadership is consistent with the pictures of churches in the New Testament. Paul's Corinthian letters show us a much more participative type of leadership based on a variety of gifts than the structured pattern in the Pastoral

Epistles. The churches in the New Testament were not carbon copies of each other but had a variety of approaches to leadership.

What is leadership? Keith Davis describes it this way: "Leadership transforms potential into reality."[4] Davis's definition can include both people and tasks. He also says that a leader "*integrates* the needs of his followers with the larger needs of his organization and the society in which it exists. Rather than *maximizing* preferred outcomes of followers, he *optimizes* these preferred outcomes through integrating them with preferred outcomes of other groups."[5]

Hersey and Blanchard distinguish between leadership and management. They propose:

> In essence, leadership is a broader concept than management. Management is thought of as a special kind of leadership in which the achievement of organizational goals is paramount. . . . Leadership occurs any time one attempts to *influence the behavior* of an individual or group, regardless of the reason.[6]

While I don't deny this distinction, I will address leadership as the leader working in the role of management.

There are several ways to look at leadership styles. One is the person or task orientation of the leader. The person/task orientations do not have to be opposites but can be integrated. In fact, Davis observes, "A manager who becomes more employee oriented does not thereby become less task oriented."[7] The style of leadership orientation does affect what gets done. Davis addresses this: "How can it be that a manager is likely to get higher productivity by emphasizing people more than task? Primarily it is because the employees achieve the task, instead of the reverse."[8]

Blake and Mouton

Robert R. Blake and Jane S. Mouton of the University of Texas developed the managerial grid illustrated on page 72.

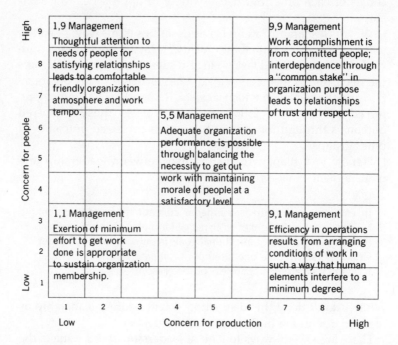

Figure 3

The managerial grid presents a person's management style relative to concerns for persons and production. The 1-9 style manager has high concerns for people but may suffer low achievement. The 9-1 is highly task oriented and usually authoritarian. Staff difficulties will likely follow for the 9-1 manager keeping achievement on a roller-coaster pattern. A management style which includes both concerns will be the most productive for an extended period.

Tannenbaum and Schmidt

Robert Tannenbaum and Warren H. Schmidt have described leadership behavior on a continuum (see Figure 4).[10]

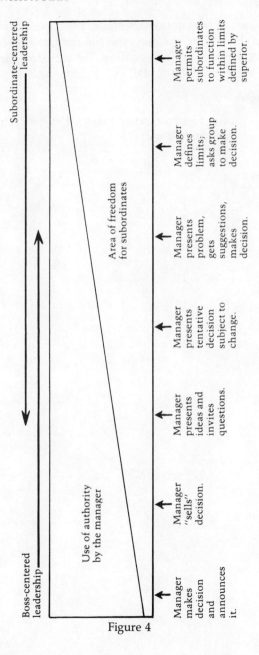

Figure 4

Boss-centered leadership

Subordinate-centered leadership

Use of authority by the manager

Area of freedom for subordinates

Manager makes decision and announces it.

Manager "sells" decision.

Manager presents ideas and invites questions.

Manager presents tentative decision subject to change.

Manager presents problem, gets suggestions, makes decision.

Manager defines limits; asks group to make decision.

Manager permits subordinates to function within limits defined by superior.

The left side of the continuum shows how an autocratic leader functions. The farther one moves to the right, the more the staff participates in planning and deciding. The more freedom the staff exercises, the more there is staff collegiality.

Jerry W. Brown

Jerry W. Brown has translated many of these concepts into what he calls "Effective Pastoral Styles."[11]

Brown's graph shows four quandrants which identify styles of pastoral leadership with regard to staff relations. Notice that he takes into account the maturity of the staff members.

Hersey and Blanchard remind us that the leader must match leadership style with the situation. The leader needs to be insightful and read the situation to know what style of leadership will be effective. The leader needs to be flexible enough to match leadership style to the situation and change styles as the situation changes. Since a new staff member will become experienced and an immature staff member should mature, the leader will need to change styles.

Leaders and Followers

There is no leadership without followers. The depth of loyalty toward the leader and confidence in the leader determines the leader's ability to lead. In any organization there are various levels of loyalty and confidence. Figure 6 shows these levels.

Level A are the loyal supporters who have confidence in the leader. I have said that these are the ones who will die for the leader. They are the followers who surround and protect the leader. A friend of mine resigned his church where there was no apparent upheaval. When I asked him why, he said he felt every pastor had to have 15 percent of the congregation with unquestioned loyalty and he didn't have that many.

Level B followers have confidence in the leader. They will fight for, but not die for, the leader.

Level C are followers, but their loyalty is more to the position of the leader than to the leader personally. They are more neutral. They won't fight for the leader, but neither are they interested in opposing the leader. Notice that this is the largest circle. Most of the people in an institution fall into this category. Their loyalty is more institutional than personal.

Level D are doubters. They lack confidence in the leader. They tend to be wary of the leader and the leader's programs.

Level E are the antagonists. They oppose the leader and seek to erode the leader's position. They will fight against the leader.

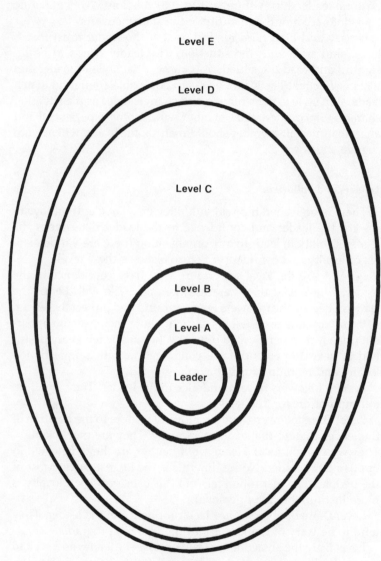

Figure 6

They may even be willing to sacrifice the institution to "get at" the leader.

People change levels as a result of two things: (1) The leader's relating, and (2) the leader's decisions. A leader has to take care of people's needs and feelings for them to move toward the inner circle. An arrogant leader or one who has poor relational skills will move people toward the outer circles. The leader's decisions will need to enhance rather than threaten the investments of the people. The leader who decides on programs which people perceive to risk their past or future investments (emotion, time, or money) erodes the force of leadership.

The leader has occasions when it is necessary to decide which people to enhance. The leader who turns to levels D and E people will make levels A and B people feel betrayed. The result will be the softening of their support of the leader.

The staff needs to be in level A or B for there to be an effective team. When a pastor begins at a church where the staff is already in place, the pastor has to earn the loyalty and confidence of the staff. Whatever their loyalty to the previous pastor, in the interim they have not had a permanent leader so they probably operated at level C. Loyalty levels A and B are not automatic with a staff; they have to be earned.

Provide Structure

An axiom of supervision is, "Structure binds anxiety." A good leader keeps anxiety at a manageable level so it does not interfere with work or relationships. Where there is too little structure, people do not know what is expected or have a time line.

Structure is like having lines on a highway. The lines indicate lanes for driving. As long as drivers adhere to their lines, driving is safe. People who need too much structure tend to be neurotic. When there is too little structure, there is confusion.

There is formal and informal structure. The formal structure is in a job description or operations manual. Formal structure defines roles of leaders. Some organizations have formal structures but operate on informal structures. When this happens, people follow traditions rather than defined procedure. Informal structure often means that someone other than the appointed leader is really in charge.

A pastor accepted a call to a church and was pleased with the clarity of his role in the church constitution. He soon found that one of the patriarchs of the church made the decisions. Informal structure was at work.

The leader provides structure. When the leader does not, someone will fill the vacuum and provide the structure. It may be another staff member or a committee. If it is not done formally, it will develop informally.

Job Description

The "job description" is a mechanism for providing structure. Every staff member merits the dignity of a job description. The responsibilities, roles, and limitations spelled out in the job description help the staff member to do the right job rather than the wrong job.

The Covenant

The leader needs to negotiate a covenant with each staff person. The covenant and job description are different. The job description sets the limits of responsibility and is generic. That is, it fits anyone who takes the job. The covenant is personal; it relates to the one person in the job. The job description is timeless, while the covenant is for a specific period. The job description relates only to the task, while the covenant pertains to the goals the staff member has with regard to the task and his or her own personal growth goals.

The covenant does not replace or supersede the job description but specifies the goals of the staff member within the scope of the job description. The covenant specifies how the staff member will meet goals in a specific time frame. A job description may state that the staff member is to be the minister of youth and administer the youth programs. The covenant may include the staff member's goals of:

1. Starting a Sunday night youth fellowship;
2. Sponsoring a spring or summer mission project;
3. Reading books on youth work;

4. Understanding developmental stages of youth;
5. Feeling more comfortable with youth.

Our Many Covenants

We make covenants with all the people with whom we have relationships. They may be clearly defined, but most are unspoken. Covenants bind people together in social and task relationships. Some of our covenants with people are the products of society (men open doors for women). Some covenants are intentional (a boy asks a girl for a date and she accepts). Some covenants come out of tradition (the pastor always visits sick parishioners). When we interrelate to people, we make or accept covenants. A major problem of human relationships is when we fail to recognize and honor a covenant—a covenant intentional, inherited, or imposed. We feel confused or betrayed when the covenant isn't honored. Wayne Oates says, "The most common cause of bad staff relationships is the failure of both the church and the staff member to get their covenantal and contractual relationship clear at the outset of their work together."[12]

Kinds of Covenants

There are three kinds of covenants: formal, informal, and tacit.[13] A formal covenant is a written document, usually stated in technical language, and is intentional. Obvious examples are documents drawn up by lawyers.

Informal covenants are less likely to be written, but they are just as intentional. Two people who agree to meet at a restaurant for lunch next Monday make an informal covenant.

Tacit covenants have hidden aspects to them. Often one or both parties never acknowledge a tacit covenant exists even though they operate by it. A tacit covenant is often the unspoken covenant which circumvents the real (formal or informal) covenant.

The tacit covenant needs to be avoided. People need to get things "on top of the table" where they can be dealt with. The tacit covenant creates problems. People operate by it when it is convenient and then revert to the real covenant, leaving others vulnerable.

The covenant is the way the leader structures relationships and goals. The institution develops the job description for whoever takes a job. The covenant is negotiated between the leader and a staff member. The covenant includes the work and growth goals of the staff member. Later they will use the covenant in the evaluation process.

Supervision

Supervision is part of the structuring of work and relationship. Supervision has to do with people. You supervise people; you administer programs. Supervision is the development of a support system for the enrichment of personhood and to assist in the performance of tasks. Both of these elements are necessary for supervision.

Supervision follows the format set up in the covenant. This should include staff and individual meetings. Staff meetings are important to coordinate work and evaluate whether tasks are helping people reach institutional goals. The leader needs to have meetings with individual staff members. Individual meetings not only relate to task but what is happening to the staff member as a person who is trying to grow.

Structure takes time but saves time. Regular supervisory meetings give the leader an opportunity to dialogue with the staff and individuals. They cut down duplication of efforts. They give staff members a time to deal with issues rather than periodically interrupting the leader. They give the staff members a sense of dignity because there is a time when they have the presence of the leader for their agenda.

Structure is the scaffolding necessary to build a building. You don't build the scaffolding for itself but for the purpose of assisting in the construction. When you build a team of staff members, you need the structure to help you do it.

Provide Planning

Planning is a major function of a leader; it's a leader's job. Organizational experts have identified five major tasks: conceptualizing, planning, organizing, directing, and controlling. These can be plotted on a graph such as the one in Figure 7.

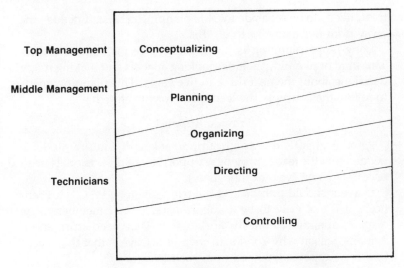

Figure 7

According to the graph, the leader has an important role in planning. While others may participate in planning, it is the leader's responsibility. A leader may share the task of planning and encourage the staff to help with the planning, but it is the leader's responsibility to provide planning. Where there is no planning, people do random or traditional tasks without well-defined goals. Even worse, individuals may do their own planning and move in different directions. This will lead to conflict, and eventually someone other than the appointed leader will emerge as the real leader.

Reginald McDonough identifies "three types of planning activities: operational planning, short-range or annual planning, and long-range or strategic planning."[14] Operational planning is the immediate task planning. This takes a great deal of time. A staff can be so caught up with operational planning that they fail to do other planning.

Short-range planning refers to goals, calendar, budgets, and needed mid-course corrections. A block of time, possibly a retreat, needs to be set aside for this planning. The staff needs time away from normal tasks to do this.

Long-range planning is a comprehensive look at the future. This kind of planning includes looking at goals and making major decisions about the next three to five years. This planning needs to follow the concepts the leader has for the church.

Provide Support

Another chapter deals with support at length, but a reminder is needed that the leader provides support. Even professionals need encouragement (yea, even leaders).

Leaders should understand the truth given by W. C. H. Prentice: "It is not easy to be a subordinate."[15] Staff members seek respect, openness, honesty, and justice. They need affirmation. A major reason why good staff members leave is that they don't find the support they need from their leader.

Fellow staff members or church members may help provide support. As important as that support is, staff members need support from their leader. And that is a leader's job.

The supportive leader will avoid arrogance and put-downs. While joking has its place, no one enjoys being the "butt" of a joke, regardless of the camaraderie. Put-downs never motivate or raise self-esteem. The leader's job is to support.

Provide Motivation

When I have spoken to groups about motivation, I often hear resistive answers:

"But they're supposed to be professional."

"They should be self-starters."

"They should be committed enough . . ."

Self-starting, committed professionals need motivation. Even leaders need motivation! One task of a leader is to provide motivation. It is true that some people are difficult to motivate. There are people in whom it is counterproductive to invest as much time as it takes to motivate them. However, there are few staff members like that.

Many books are written on motivation. It is a favorite subject in management journals and seminars. When I lead a seminar and ask about supervisory problems, motivation is always mentioned. It is a leader's issue.

While we understand that motivation is a complex issue, the simple "Golden Rule" of our Lord is at the heart of motivation. Doing to others as we would have them do to us is the key to motivation if we are insightful enough to put ourselves in their place. Harry Levinson[16] challenges managers to examine their assumptions. We cannot assume that others want what we want. We can fulfill the Golden Rule only when we understand what the other person wants or needs. We want others to meet our needs, so the Golden Rule means that we must meet the needs of others.

In American society we are material oriented, so our first temptation is to explain motivation in terms of money. However, as important as money is, most people in our society have access to enough money that it is not a positive motivation. Most people on church staffs are not highly motivated by money or they would not be on a church staff but in a higher-paying vocation. Something else motivates them.

People are different, so they are motivated by different things. The Myers-Briggs Type Indicator and Bi-Polar Seminars point out differences in the approach of people to life. Some people are motivated by ideas, others by people, programs, or things. An idea person can be turned on by a philosophical statement which leaves a program person cold.

When people discuss motivation, they usually refer to Abraham Maslow.[17] He related motivation to a hierarchy of human needs. Understanding human needs is basic in motivation, although it may not be easy to move from this general conceptualization to specific implementation.

Maslow identified five human needs: physiological, security, social, ego, and self-realization. The lower-order needs (physiological and security) have to be met before the higher-order needs (social, ego, and self-fulfillment) are relevant. After all, a starving man cares little for a bowling trophy. The lower-order needs are usually satisfied by economic means (five dollars for a meal), while the higher-order needs are satisfied more through symbolic actions (to be listed in *Who's Who*).

When we apply Maslow's ideas, we will have to determine at what need level a staff member is operating. Also, the need levels are not clear-cut in life so that more than one is always relevant. The physiological must be maintained in order to deal with self-esteem (ego) needs. The leader who develops a staff into a team provides for belonging (social) needs. A good team affirms its members, meeting self-esteem (ego) needs. A good leader stimulates the team members to grow, be creative, and make significant contributions which feed the self-realization needs.

Frederick Herzberg is another celebrated researcher of motivation. His approach was to ask employees to think of a time when they felt good about their jobs, moments when they had bad feelings about their jobs, and the conditions which were operative. He called the dissatisfiers "maintainance factors" (or "hygiene") and the satisfiers "motivational factors." A graph of the results of interviews is shown in Figure 8.[18]

The significance of his research is that some things hinder motivation but they are not motivating factors themselves. For example, company policy can create problems, but good company policy does not motivate. Achievement is motivational. Of course, they may be related. A person may not be able to achieve where there are poor policies, but the perception of what satisfies is achievement, not good policies.

R. Lofton Hudson, pastor, counselor, and author, has been an important mentor for me. We once flew together to Virginia where we were to speak at a pastor's conference. I took the opportunity to ask him about motivation. He suggested four motivators: guilt, shame, reality, and love. With some adjustment, I have found that these help me understand motivation.

Guilt is the feeling stimulated in us because we are responsible for wrongdoing and are to blame. Ministers have motivated (sometimes manipulated) people through guilt. The human soul has a felt need to "even the score" so that when a person feels guilty, he can be motivated by someone's appealing to the guilt. One of the major catalysts of the Protestant Reformation was the institutionalizing of guilt which led Tetzel and others to sell indulgences.

Guilt is a powerful force in the human soul. The person who

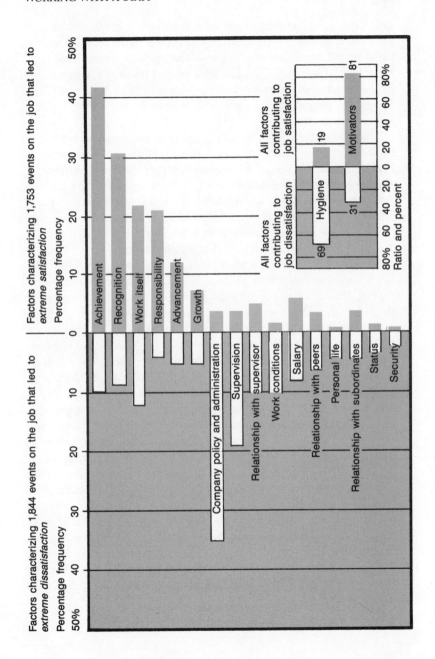

Factors characterizing 1,844 events on the job that led to *extreme dissatisfaction*

Percentage frequency

Factors characterizing 1,753 events on the job that led to *extreme satisfaction*

Percentage frequency

Achievement
Recognition
Work itself
Responsibility
Advancement
Growth
Company policy and administration
Supervision
Relationship with supervisor
Work conditions
Salary
Relationship with peers
Personal life
Relationship with subordinates
Status
Security

All factors contributing to job dissatisfaction

All factors contributing to job satisfaction

Hygiene
69
31

Motivators
81
19

Ratio and percent

raises old guilt feelings which were resolved or creates improper guilt feelings does a dangerous disservice. Guilt can bring depression, destruction of personal relationship, erosion of self-esteem, and suicide. Guilt can be a proper motivator when there has been blameworthy behavior which needs to be dealt with. When it is proper, guilt motivation will enrich the guilty person, not the motivator.

Shame may be confused with guilt. Shame has to do with dishonor and humiliation without the presence of wrongdoing. Shame is used in "what if" situations rather than real situations. A mother uses shame when she says, "Son, I want to be proud of you; I hope you never act like Johnny." You never have acted like Johnny but you are motivated by shame not to act like Johnny. While shame is much misused, it is also valuable to help people see the folly which certain actions would bring.

Hudson said that some people (especially sociopaths) have little or no sense of guilt or shame. They can only be motivated by reality. When such persons do wrong, you can only motivate them by showing them the unpleasant consequences of their actions such as imprisonment, injury, lawsuits, or ill health.

Reality as a motivator is the use of fear. We have heard the horror stories of evangelists holding people over the fires of hell to motivate them to "walk the aisle." Wayne Oates once told me that people no longer have a fear of hell but now fear sexual impotence. I was inexperienced in counseling at the time and found it to be a curious statement. Since then the Masters-Johnson clinic for sexual dysfunction has gained wide attention. Recently newspaper articles relate that people have become less promiscuous because of the fear of AIDS and herpes. The implication is that their lessened promiscuity is not because of guilt or shame but fear.

Fear can be a proper motivation. There are dangers we should fear. Children without normal fear seldom survive. The exaggeration of fear is manipulative, and improper fear can do serious damage. The child may develop an obsession which will be unreasonable in adult life. Undue sexual fears may lead to adult dysfunction.

Love is a great motivator. Love for children and mates have motivated people to make enormous sacrifices. Love for God or country has motivated people to martyrdom and heroism. Love as a motivator is why John 3:16 is such a popular Scripture.

Love is an improper motivator when the object of love is wrong. A minister who asks people to take church responsibilities on the basis of friendship has cheated the volunteers. The proper motivation is to do something because the person loves the Lord, not the minister.

A seminar participant once suggested that greed ought to be added as a motivator. It is true that people are motivated by greed. The apostle Paul understood the nature of greed when he said, "The love of money is the root of all evil" (1 Tim. 6:10, KJV). Greed is a kind of misplaced love. Greed is not so much a motivating force from without as it is a compulsion from within.

I add another motivator that Hudson did not suggest: hope. People respond to dreams. As long as a group shares a dream, they are highly motivated. Bob Dale wrote a book, *To Dream Again*,[19] which is a testimony to the power of shared dreams. Churches have dreamed of a new building or ministries and have made enormous sacrifices to fulfill the dream. A staff that dreams together works together.

The person who motivates by offering false hope is a charlatan. We have seen hope used as a motivation for the terminally ill by charlatans. False prophets are purveyors of false hope.

There are two things a leader can do to motivate people. First, the leader needs to be motivated. When you demonstrate an exceptionally high energy level, you will energize others.

Second, the leader can give people attention. If you put ministry in management terms, ministry is a people industry rather than a product industry. People respond to attention. The Hawthorne experiment was one of the most enlightening management research projects. Elton Mayo of the Harvard Graduate School of Business Administration and his team performed experiments on the motivation of employees at the Western Electric plant in Hawthorne, Illinois. They divided the employees into two groups, an experimental group which worked under varying conditions and a control group for whom nothing was changed. As changes were made with the experimental group, their productivity went up. But so did the productivity of the control group. When left without changes, production returned to normal. With every innovation in the experimental group, the researchers saw the pattern repeat. Finally, after a year and a half, they took away the innovations, such as a shorter work week, scheduled breaks, and company lunches. The researchers expected the psychological impact to reduce productivity. Instead, productivity went to an all-time high. The researchers found that the secret was not in the production aspects but the human situation. As a result of the profuse attention given them by the experimenters, the employees felt that they were an important part of the company.

During discussion time in a seminar, I ignored Ted, one of the participants. Whenever Ted spoke, I looked at the floor or at someone else. When he finished, rather than responding to Ted, I acknowledged and interacted with the next person. After three attempts, Ted never spoke again. At the conclusion of the discussion and while the group was still together, I asked Ted what he had experienced. He acknowledged that he felt put down and was confused and angry. He said he finally gave up trying to make any contribution. (He was relieved to find out that it was a deliberate experiment and nothing was wrong with him.) We motivate people with attention even when there is no logical need to give it. Without attention, people give up.

Your job as leader is to find people's needs, help them to become part of the dream, model energetic leadership, and give them attention. Your job is to provide motivation.

Provide Communication

One day my daughter came home from grade school crying and angry. Her mother inquired about the problem. The teacher had called my daughter's best friend a horse. Just because her friend had a cold, my daughter said, she was not a horse. Her mother patiently explained the difference between "horse" and "hoarse." Communication is a difficult enterprise.

Problems in Communicating

Supervisors and staff persons can expect communication problems. Communication is mysterious enough when both parties try to make it work. Greater problems arise in supervision where there is inadequate structure, resistance, or unclear goals. Communication problems also are compounded when supervision is cross-cultural.

Listening is a major problem in communication. Public schools spend millions of dollars teaching remedial as well as regular courses in reading. We spend more hours a day listening, but who has ever taken a course on listening?

Good listening can vastly improve the communicating process. One should actively listen rather than merely sit in the geographical locale of the speaker. Ask, "Am I spending as much energy and concentrating as much when I listen as when I speak?" The supervisor who does not listen to staff personnel with concentration can expect to be heard with the same indifference. One of the best ways a supervisor can teach communication is by modeling listening. Supervisors who listen communicate caring and the idea that they think the supervisee is important. Good listening is not only hearing words but receiving feeling behind those words. Words do not always bear the message; feeling behind the words may be a cry for help. Good listening is accomplished with the ears of the mind and the ears of the heart.

Everyone communicates within a context. The context includes family and cultural background, goals, education, and existing pressures. A supervisor within five years of retirement works from a different context than the twenty-five-year-old person in the first ministry position who dreams about future job possibilities. An Anglo comes from an entirely different context than a black or Hispanic mission person. Words may not mean the same to supervisor and staff personnel; each reacts differently to ideas. Regional idioms may cause misunderstanding.

Wendell Belew, director of Missions Ministries Division of the Home Mission Board, tells about sending a seminary student from Mississippi to preach in the hills of Kentucky. He instructed the student to stop at a certain place, pick up an elderly woman, and take her to church. Later that week, when Belew asked the woman how she liked the young man, he was surprised to find out that she had been offended. The young man had offered to "carry her" to church. The Deep South idiom of "carrying" people resulted in a gross communication problem.

Authority can create or alleviate communication problems. Observing an associate pastor lead a seminar, I noticed no one responded when he asked for feedback. After an hour, the pastor affirmed what he had heard from the associate and from that point there was stimulating dialogue. Titles, over-under relationships, personal charisma, and forced relationships create communication problems. The supervisor should anticipate communication difficulties with staff members when a supervisor is assigned a supervisory role. The difficulties are not insurmountable, but they do need to be addressed early in the supervisory relationship. Supervisors need to offer special opportunities for the staff to relate both their ideas and feelings about the supervisory roles, the ground rules, and relationships. Supervisors should also promise to hear and seriously consider staff members when they communicate. Supervisors also need to clarify boundaries due to system requirements.

The setting influences communication. If the session occurs in the supervisor's office, the supervisor's role and authority is heightened because the person is on the supervisor's turf. The desk behind which the supervisor sits communicates that something is between the two persons. Free-flowing communication occurs in a neutral place, or at least one not closely identified with the supervisor. They should sit facing one another with no barriers in between. A man who is a sought-after expert in his field told of a job interview during which the dean sat behind his desk the whole time. The man perceived the dean as arrogant and impersonal. Consequently, he turned down the job offer.

The supervisor is responsible to examine the communication occurring between himself/herself and staff personnel. Transactional Analysis, especially the ego states, may provide a good method for evaluating the communication process. The supervisor will need to ask, for example, "Am I operating out of the 'critical parent' ego state—and from what ego state is the staff personnel responding?" Supervisors may ascertain their movement from one ego state to the other. They should also try to determine that of the personnel.

The Critical Part of Communication

The following model shows the options, factors, and problems in the path of communication between two people.

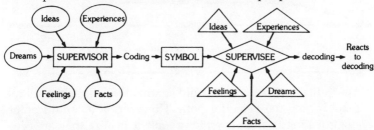

Both supervisor and supervisee operate in each situation with their own ideas, facts, experiences, feelings, and dreams. Although the model has been drawn with all elements of equal importance, in reality the elements may be more like the following model.

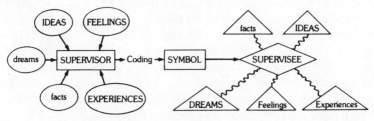

Communications under these circumstances might appear impossible—or miraculous. The supervisor codes communication and creates a symbol which is passed on to the staff personnel. Because of the variant frames of reference, no symbol is the perfect bearer of communication and a symbol may be counterproductive. At the same time, the symbol may be a way of refusing to disclose information. The phrase, "he hid his feelings" may also apply to language which may prevent communication as well as permit it. With all of these possibilities of noncommunication or miscommunication, the supervisor and staff personnel need to double-check what is said in order to ensure communication. The following model shows this graphically.

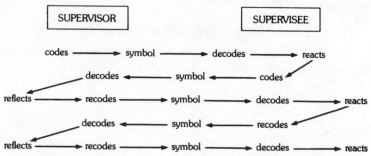

Theoretically this process could continue indefinitely until the symbol means the same for both. However, at a certain point, enough testing has occurred for people to realize they are communicating adequately or will never be able to communicate. Misunderstanding can be minimized by patiently testing the communication process.

Body Language

Each person may interpret body language to some extent but not always be conscious of it. We have heard people say, "I knew he wasn't telling me the truth because he couldn't look me in the eye." People communicate by what they do with their bodies as well as by their words. They communicate with the way they look at us, whether they cross their arms or legs, whether they lean toward or away from us, and where they sit in relation to us. Usually people are unconscious of their body language.

Once a man led a group conference on supervision. After the conference, I apologized for one person whose inappropriate remarks demonstrated that he did not understand what was being said. The leader said to me, "Yes, I noticed you cleared your throat every time he started to speak." The leader had picked up my unconscious body language. I could have offered some excuse about sinus drainage, but the truth was that the leader had picked up my response when this particular person spoke.

In a nonthreatening supervisory relationship, supervisors

could interrupt conversation to discuss the meaning of any observed body language. This could sensitize the supervisor and staff personnel to intense feelings or resistance.

Formal and Informal Communication

Behind-the-scenes diplomatic negotiations often further international understandings more than the formal statements made by diplomats. Formal statements may be made to save face and hold traditional positions. Behind the scenes, diplomats may deal with issues in a realistic way.

Supervisors and staff personnel will find these same conditions in formal and informal communication. Informal communication—over lunch, for example—may help solve problems in ways that formal supervisory sessions do not. It is not the meal which makes a session informal, but the consciousness that the participants are no longer in a formal setting.

Structured Communication

Structure communication by structuring the format. Oral communication is faster and allows for observation of body language. It is more spontaneous, less precise, and may open opportunities for game playing. If communication problems arise with oral data, supervisors should request written data.

Supervisors and staff personnel can structure checking out communication. The supervisor may need to ask the staff personnel, "What did you understand me to say?" Staff personnel may answer, "I understood you to say . . ." Feedback offers time to check if what was said was appropriately communicated. (Staff personnel should not say to the supervisor, "What you said was" but, "This is what I heard you say.")

Communication is the primary vehicle for the supervisor. When the vehicle is faulty, adequate supervision cannot occur. Supervision may even be harmful rather than helpful without adequate communication.

Provide Delegation

Where there is no delegation, there is no reason for a staff. The staff deserves the dignity of delegation—real delegation. It should not be the kind where the leader takes back the responsibility.

That kind of delegating has been called "rubber-band" delegation because it snaps back to the delegator. Real delegation provides legitimate roles for the staff.

Why Leaders Hesitate to Delegate

If delegation is what a staff is about, why do leaders hesitate to delegate? But many leaders hesitate.

Perfectionism is one reason. Many leaders are compulsive perfectionists who need every detail polished. The perfectionist has difficulty getting everything done which needs to be done. What perfectionists do will be polished, but they leave many areas untouched. Perfectionists who cannot delegate are not really effective leaders.

A nonperfectionist leader may realize that he or she can do it better than a staff person. The leader has experience, maturity, and skills beyond the staff member. But what is the purpose of having a staff if the leader follows this philosophy? The time and energy a staff member has to put into a task expands the work of the church even if the staff member can't do it as well as the leader.

The leader may not have confidence in the staff member. This is a "Catch-22" situation since staff members can only prove and improve themselves by taking on responsibilities. The job of the leader is not to match responsibilities to the level of ability the staff member possesses. Gradually the level of responsibility can be increased.

The leader may lack confidence in himself or herself to direct others in delegation. Someone asks us how to get to an office and after trying to tell them, we end up saying, "I've got to go that way; I'll take you." We may have difficulty directing.

The fear of losing control is a leader's problem in delegating. The leader has always done the task, and to turn it over to a staff member may make it appear as loss of control. The leader with a need for high control has difficulty delegating and may end up being the "harried executive." When the leader delegates and the staff member grows in the responsibility, the leader may be threatened by the appearance that the staff member is a rival.

Risk taking is difficult for some leaders. Any delegation involves risks, and the fear of risk taking may make the leader reluctant to delegate.

A leader may refuse to delegate a task because the task is an attractive one. Although the leader may not have the time, he or she may enjoy doing the task and not give it up.

Overcoming Resistance to Delegation

The leader may have problems delegating because staff members are reluctant to accept delegation. After all, it may be safer to ask the leader and not be caught "holding the bag." The staff member may fear criticism from the leader or others. The leader will need to provide an environment for acceptance to overcome this resistance. At the beginning the leader may need to keep in close touch with the staff member to build confidence and alleviate fear.

Resistance from the staff member may come from a lack of knowledge or resources. Leaders are always teachers. They need to give information to the staff member. I have seen leaders play "hide and seek," daring the staff members to find the information. Delegated tasks are only as effective as the available resources. The staff member should not be held accountable if the leader cannot provide the resources.

When staff members already have more than they can do, they will resist delegation. If the leader has too much to do, there is no profit in delegating to an overloaded staff member.

The staff member may lack self-confidence. This is heightened if the leader does not give positive feedback on good work done. The good leader does not forget the human element in delegating.

Characteristics of a Good Delegator

The good delegator is a good communicator who can clearly define what needs to be done, the time line, and the process of accountability. The effective delegator will listen to the staff member repeat the assignment to see if there has been clear communication.

Receptivity to the ideas of others makes a good delegator. Delegation is usually a negotiated issue where the staff member has input into the methods and maybe even the goals and time line.

The effective delegator is mature enough to see mistakes and charge them off as a worthwhile investment in people. It is counterproductive for a delegator to rant and rave about mistakes. A good leader helps the staff work through their mistakes.

Having patience and tolerance enhances the effectiveness of a delegator. The good leader brings the staff along at a quickening pace rather than impatiently expecting everything at the beginning. Fathers are often guilty of taking a tool from a child's hand and doing the task, rather than patiently waiting and coaching the child.

The Process of Delegation

There are steps which enhance delegation. First, agree on the task, its goals, and how it will be measured. If you can't clearly define the goal, don't delegate.

Second, turn over the authority to do the task. Delegation without authority won't work and will only lead to frustration.

Third, communicate the delegation and authority clearly to the rest of the staff and congregation. Without this, the staff members face difficulties.

Fourth, establish a monitoring process. At the beginning, let the staff member know when you want reports on the project.

Fifth, maintain a proper atmosphere so the task can be done. Your support and acceptance will make delegation work.

Sixth, evaluate the work. Let the staff members know how you assess the work. This will help them feel that you pay attention and clarify how they can work with you on the next assignment.

Delegation is at the heart of leadership, but the leader must not be so mystic as to look only at the task. There is a person involved. Delegation depends on human needs being met.

Provide Evaluation

Christ is the Great Shepherd and pastors are the undershepherds. God is the final Judge, but leaders have the responsibility of temporal evaluation. Staff members function best when there is evaluation, so they know where they are and whether they are meeting expectations.

Evaluation can be capricious and cruel, or it can be an affirming and growing experience. Accountability is a reality of life. Without it, we will not do our best or know whether we have failed or achieved. Jesus gave several parables emphasizing human accountability (for example, Matt. 21:33-43; 24:45-51; 25:14-30).

Evaluation needs to be structured so it will be helpful instead of hurtful. One reason for the covenant is to provide the structure for evaluation. The staff member is accountable according to the covenant. It is the instrument which helps the leader in evaluation. The covenant also limits the areas of accountability to provide fairness for the staff member.

Evaluation happens each time the leader has a conference with the staff member. The leader should indicate whether the staff member is on target. The major evaluation should be no surprise to the staff member.

The covenant should set a specific time for evaluation. This should be a formal time in which the evaluation is the sole agenda. If the leader has kept notes, the evaluation can be specific. The leader will want to give the staff member an opportunity to respond to the evaluation. The evaluation is important in writing or renegotiating the future covenant.

The use of the evaluation needs to be clear. Will it be for promotion or raises? Is it only for the personal growth of the staff member? Will it be used to determine future employment or a future recommendation?

There *will* be evaluation. The only question is, Will it be helpful or hurtful? Unless the staff members can get feedback from evaluation, they can't hope to improve. We always evaluate. The first moment we meet someone, we have an opinion. Only when a person gets honest feedback can the person profit.

Much of this book has emphasized relationships. I hope this chapter has demonstrated the need for the human element. Being the leader of a staff means, above all, relating to people. Any kind of staff structure only serves to structure relationships in a productive way. Leaders who rely on mechanisms and organization alone will not be effective. Good leaders help people grow and treat them with reverence and dignity.

Notes

1. Keith Davis, *Human Behavior at Work*, Fourth Edition (New York: McGraw-Hill, 1972), p. 107.

2. Paul Hersey and Ken Blanchard, *Management of Organizational Behavior* (Englewood Cliffs, N.J.: Prentice-Hall, 1982), pp. 83, 345.

3. Ibid.

4. Davis, *Human Behavior at Work*, pp. 100, 584.

5. Ibid., p. 101.

6. Hersey and Blanchard, *Management of Organizational Behavior*, p. 3.

7. Davis, *Human Behavior at Work*, p. 112.

8. Ibid., p. 113.

9. Robert R. Blake and Jane S. Mouton, "Management Facades," *Advanced Management Journal*, July, 1966, p. 31.

10. Robert Tannenbaum and Warren H. Schmidt, "How to Choose a Leadership Pattern," ed. Ralph F. Lewis (*Harvard Business Review*, May-June, 1973), p. 164.

11. Jerry W. Brown, *Church Staffs that Win*, p. 35.

12. Wayne Oates, "Factors Hindering Effective Staff Relationships" *Search* (Summer, 1971), p. 24.

13. For more on covenants see, *The Supervision of Mission Personnel*, by Doran McCarty, published by the Home Mission Board of the Southern Baptist Convention (1350 Spring St. NW, Atlanta)

14. Reginald McDonough, *Search* (Spring, 1984), p. 34.

15. W. C. H. Prentice "Understanding Leadership," *Paths Toward Personal Progress: Leaders Are Made, Not Born* (*Harvard Business Review*, 1983), p. 4.

16. Harry Levinson, "Asinine Attitudes Toward Motivation" (*Harvard Business Review*, Jan.-Feb. 1973).

17. Abraham Maslow, *Motivation and Personality* (New York: Harper & Row, 1954).

18. Frederick Herzberg, "One More Time: How Do You Motivate Employees?" (*Harvard Business Review*, Jan.-Feb., 1968), p. 57.

19. Robert Dale, *To Dream Again* (Nashville: Broadman Press, 1981).

This chapter is an adaptation of chapter 13, "Communicating," in the book *The Supervision of Mission Personnel* by Doran McCarty. The art on pages 92-93 is reproduced with permission of the Home Mission Board.

7
Working with Volunteers

Two people I interviewed about their work with volunteers gave me two stories poles apart. The first leader enthusiastically told me that she had 120 volunteers who worked at her center at least one day a month. The second leader said that he had had about a dozen volunteers over the years but only two or three showed up anymore.

Volunteers: A Way of Life

A democratic society depends upon volunteers. Volunteers are a necessity for a church. A major function of a church leader is to work with volunteers. In most churches that have no paid staff, the major leadership responsibility of the pastor is to supervise a volunteer staff.

Volunteers make up the choir, the Sunday School teachers and officers, and the committees. The volunteers are the real church staff. *All of the principles about working with a staff in the last chapter apply to working with volunteers!* This statement is often rejected by the retort, "You can't supervise volunteers because they're not paid." Volunteers get something out of what they do or they wouldn't volunteer. Money is not the only reason staff members work for churches; they also join a staff for fulfillment. The volunteer joins a staff not for money, but for fulfillment. If you refused to pay staff members, you would anticipate that they would resign. Staff members leave when they are paid but lack fulfillment or anticipate greater fulfillment elsewhere. You have to provide volunteers with the fulfillment they seek or they will quit. Volunteers experience the Lord's words: "Man shall not live by bread alone" (Matt. 4:4, KJV). A leader can supervise volunteers as long as volunteers receive what they need from leaders. The difference in supervising volunteers and staff members is situational, not a difference in principle.

Volunteerism is a way of life because of the enormity of the leader's responsibilities. The leader has to delegate to volunteers. The pastor can't teach all the Sunday School classes, do all the visitation, care for the building, and keep the treasurer's books.

The leader also needs people who have skills the leader lacks. A church needs volunteers with skills in music, management, finances, cooking, carpentry, and mechanics beyond the skills of the leader.

Volunteerism is a way of life because that is the way people grow. The leader who tries to do it all robs would-be volunteers of an opportunity for personal and Christian growth. People do not grow sitting as much as they grow serving.

The use of volunteers increases investment in the cause of Christ. When people do volunteer work, they invest time and emotions, if not money, in the church. Investments create interest. Investments create concern and the desire for a church to achieve. People promote and protect their investments and volunteers do those things for the church where they serve. Volunteers become part of the team when they invest in the church. They develop loyalties and make further investments. I have seen church members who made little financial contribution begin to give financial support when they started investing their lives through a volunteer responsibility.

Who Are Volunteers?

Virginia is a volunteer. Although she is not paid, she works for her church as many as twenty hours a week. Several times late at night the pastor has called her to help with a youth who has gotten into trouble.

Margaret called her pastor. She said, "I've heard about the Martins' troubles. If I can help, let me know."

Volunteers are concerned people. They want to help. Giving volunteers an opportunity to serve helps them. Virginia is a former social worker who has expertise which she doesn't want to waste when there are so many needs in the community. Margaret is a loving, caring person whose nest is empty, but she still reaches out to care for people.

Volunteers are people who have needs. Leaders minister to them by meeting those needs. The effective leader will be perceptive to the needs of the volunteers as well as the needs of the church organization. The ineffective leader will assume that the volunteer only wants to meet organizational needs and ignore the volunteer's needs. Several problems surface when the leader is insensitive to the volunteer's needs. The leader may give the volunteer the wrong job. The leader may not be able to motivate the volunteer. The volunteer may function poorly or pursue his or her own agenda rather than the goals of the church.

Look for the volunteer's needs. An elderly widow may need attention to dispel the loneliness of her house emptied of human warmth except for her haunting memories. Persons may impulsively volunteer because of their perceived need for absolution for a sin. Others may need acceptance which they don't find in social clubs, at school, or at work. There are neurotics who have a compulsion to straighten things out. Others need fulfillment in their lives and volunteer in order to become all God wants them to be.

The leader who overlooks the needs of volunteers is borrowing trouble. Persons who need absolution may soon feel better and quit. Or they may even feel more guilty and become dysfunctional. The leader may not want the problems a neurotic will create, even though the neurotic is gifted and energetic.

Whatever the volunteer's need, the effective leader will have to contribute to fulfilling it. That is the pay for the volunteer. The leader may have to discover the volunteers' needs because the volunteers may not be conscious of their needs or able to articulate them.

The Process of Working with Volunteers

"When I need somebody, I'll ask." That was a statement of a young pastor who didn't want to waste time talking about supervising volunteers. Later I heard him complain and admonish that his church needed a spiritual revival because the members wouldn't serve sacrificially. I suspect that the two statements are related.

The leader with a good volunteer staff has a good volunteer program. Such a program doesn't just happen; the leader provides a process for its development. Although they may be called different things, there are identifiable steps in an effective process.

Step 1: Develop a Program

Define Goals

Discriminating volunteers don't give the leader a blank check for their services. They want their services to go to a program which has purpose, integrity, and resources. The effective leader begins to develop a program by setting goals which are specific, attainable, and measurable. The leader can communicate those kinds of goals.

Prepare Plans

Once leaders define goals, they begin to plan. Different volunteers can help with various parts of the plan. Volunteers need the dignity of knowing the goals and how they fit into the overall plans. Without plans they are only good intentions.

Develop Job Descriptions

The leader can write job descriptions which fit the tasks the plans call for. Yes, volunteers need job descriptions. They are no less part of a team than a paid staff member. A job description tells a volunteer that a job is important and has been thought through. Every volunteer deserves the dignity of a job description. If the leader has a job description for a volunteer, it means that the leader has a handle on the job and can communicate it clearly. A volunteer, as well as a paid staff member, can interfere with a job that is not his or hers. Without a job description, the leader will have trouble trying to handle the situation.

Step 2: Develop Personnel

No program will be better than the people doing the program. Conversely, a well-planned program may fail if the wrong people or unprepared people work in it. Again, the human element is paramount.

Build Expectations

The leader builds expectations. Betty said to her sister, "Come on down to the center with me. We never really do anything but visit." Low expectations will assure low productivity. Build expectations before recruiting. Use the grapevine to let people know what you will expect. People who don't want to give serious service will not bother to volunteer. Volunteers who are looking for significant service will begin with a strong commitment to contribute.

Recruit

The leader's job is to sell. While an article may be put in the church bulletin about the need for a volunteer, the leader should court volunteers and sell them on the jobs. Even when persons approach you about taking a job, they need to feel wanted rather than that they are getting the job by default. Not everyone is like you; some are shy and are "cautious lovers." They will respond enthusiastically to a request but would never be forward enough to ask. They may make excellent volunteers.

Recruit people who can manage your specific job descriptions. Effectiveness in a volunteer program is matching the right people to the right tasks. They may not teach Sunday School classes but are the right ones for other ministries. If you have a job description, you may share it with someone and ask if they know who would be good at the task. Don't be afraid to ask. The person may be a mayor, professor, or millionaire and is waiting for a way to serve with his or her unique gifts.

Don't get in a rut with your recruiting. Many young people can help. Retirees are looking for meaningful tasks. New members seek a way to start serving. There are some ministries where you need the expertise of professionals who are not in your church.

Train

When you recruit, promise training. Training is for everyone. An orientation may be all some need, but it is important to help them feel there is a team and they are part of it. Others need skill training in their job. You may have done the task so many times that it seems easy to do. (Don't fall into the trap of saying, "Anybody can do it.") They may have skills that need to be readjusted to the particular task.

There is resistance to training. One reason is the problem of time. A volunteer may feel he or she has time to serve but not time to train. An axiom of supervision is: "If they won't train, they won't serve." Experience has borne this out. Some feel that training is a "put-down." (Do they think I don't know enough to . . . ?") You can help by taking an affirming approach, such as saying that you want them to have a good experience, so you will provide a special opportunity as they start. Remember, you are not dealing with only one person, but a team of people. Those who take training will resent those who do not. Those who will not take training will likely not be team members.

Covenant

Volunteers deserve a covenant which indicates their task and personal growth goals. (See the previous chapter for a discussion of covenants.) The covenant will help both of you know whether the volunteer is on target throughout the period of the job.

Step 3: Work at the Task

All roads lead to this step—the task. There are ways the leader can help during this time.

Delegate

The leader delegates to the volunteer. The task delegated should be significant, not "make-do" work. The task needs to be consistent with the job description and the readiness and maturity of the volunteer. (For more on delegation, see the previous chapter.)

Initiate

Help the volunteers get started. You may go with them the first day to acquaint them with the setting and give moral support. There is a psychological barrier in doing something the first time.

Provide

The effective leader provides volunteers with what they need to do the job. Providing includes supplies, data, money, and authority. One of the most common complaints from volunteers is that no one provided the resources they needed to do the job.

Motivate

Volunteers are human; they need continued motivation. Leaders may spend all their energy motivating people to volunteer, and spend no energy motivating volunteers on the job. (See the previous chapter for a discussion on motivation.)

Communicate

Volunteers don't like to feel that their supervisor is an absentee landlord. They want to hear from their supervisor about their job and how the whole program is going. The leader is unwise who does not set up regular times to get feedback from the volunteer. The volunteer needs to debrief, express feelings, and know someone listens. It is in the leader's interest to have communication in order to monitor the program.

The communication will be more helpful if it is on a regular basis. Monitoring is less threatening if it is structured. The axiom applies: Structure binds anxiety.

Crisis Management

The leader has to deal with crises in the work from time to time. The volunteer becomes ill, materials don't arrive, behavior problems arise among the participants—these are some of the crises which a leader will face. The communication and monitoring will help detect some of these issues before they become crises.

Step 4: Evaluation

The volunteer deserves evaluation, and the job demands it. A time for evaluation should be set when the covenant is made. While some evaluation happens as the work goes on, a specific evaluation is important. (See the previous chapter for a discussion of evaluation.)

Step 5: Recycling

Renegotiate

Evaluation provides insight as to whether the task and volunteer should continue. If the decision is to continue, the leader and volunteer should renegotiate the covenant and probably make adjustments in the task.

Retrain

Volunteers may profit from additional training, having found that there are areas in which they could improve. Or the job may have changed to require additional skills.

Volunteers are important. They deserve a leader's tender, loving care. The leader's work will not succeed without volunteers. The volunteers are not machines to be plugged in, but human persons to be cared for and ministered to.

8
Confrontation

"Reverend Jenkins, you've been counseling Debbie for several weeks and I don't know what is going on. She is a teenager, living in my home, and I care about her. I want to know what this is all about. She won't tell me; I want *you* to tell me."

This is confrontation. Debbie's mother intentionally initiates a conversation with Reverend Jenkins in order to create change; she wants information she doesn't have. Of course, confrontation may lead to conflict.

Many stories in the Bible are about confrontation. Jethro confronted Moses ("What you are doing is not good") in order to get Moses to change the way he administered the affairs of the Hebrew people (Ex. 18:17). Nathan confronted David about his sin with Bathsheba with his famous parable (2 Sam. 12:1ff.). Jesus confronted both disciples (Matt. 26:52) and foes (Matt. 23:13-15). Paul confronted Peter (Gal. 2:11). Without confrontation, the history of God's people would have been different.

Why We Confront

Growth

Growth comes through confrontation. During my years directing the programs of Doctor of Ministry candidates, I have observed that their personal and professional growth have come when supervisors confronted. When left unconfronted, they continued in their unproductive patterns. There was almost always pain and suffering in the confrontation—both in the supervisor and doctoral candidate. Suffering was the price of confrontation and growth.

Care

Why do we confront when there are risks of suffering and conflicts? We confront because we care. We care for people, for truth,
for ideals, for organizations, and things. David Augsburger
coined the term "carefronting."[1] When we do not care (or care
enough), we do not confront. I was sitting in La Guardia Airport
waiting for my flight. Two strangers sat down across from me and
one said to the other, "I see we land in Dover. That's in Pennsyl-
vania, isn't it?" The second responded, "No, it's in New Jersey." I
had never seen them before and in five minutes, I would never
see them again. I didn't care enough to confront and inform them
that Dover is in Delaware. (Had they been the pilots, I probably
would have said something.)

My wife is a gentle person who finds it difficult to confront.
One of our daughters had broken her curfew several nights and
my wife and I decided we needed to confront her about it. I knew
the burden of confrontation would be on me. To my surprise, my
wife initiated the confrontation with love but intensity. I learned
something. Anyone who cares enough can and will confront.
Augsburger is right; it is *carefronting*.

Change

We confront because we want change. We want to change the
status quo or we want to rid ourselves of the threat to the status
quo. Change adds to the suffering of confrontation because of the
axiom "change means loss." While we may gain from change and
never want to go back to the way things were, loss comes with
change. Confrontation is the way to bring about the changes we
believe beneficial and worth the suffering and loss. Everything
changes, but without confrontation, the changes may be undesir-
able.

Why We Don't Confront

Proverbs 27:5 says, "Better is open rebuke than hidden love."
Given the truth of that Scripture, we still often avoid confronting
others. Why? One reason we avoid confrontation (and conflict) is
because we have been taught that "it's not nice." This feeling is

part of the emotional baggage we carry from childhood. Much of this attitude is cultural. I have noticed that my Italian friends have less trouble with confrontation. They can confront intensely and love no less.

We don't confront because of the myth of peace and unity. Peace becomes silence and passivity, which proves there is unity. Quietude doesn't assure unity; nor does unity mean total abstinence from confronting. In fact, confronting may be a step toward peace and unity.

Fear keeps us from confronting. We fear getting hurt or hurting. Healthy people aren't so fragile but that they can tolerate confronting or being confronted. People don't fall to pieces easily. On the contrary, confronting may strengthen and toughen.

Self-esteem gets in the way. Confronting may erode our sense of "OKness." Our self-image may be that we are pleasant and easy to get along with and confronting someone might damage that self-image.

We may not confront because it is not worth it to us. Given the reality of risk and suffering when we confront, we don't care enough to confront.

Qualities of a Good Confronter

All are not equal in the skill of confronting. Some people have the qualities it takes to be a good confronter and others do not. There are at least six characteristics of a good confronter.

Care

Caring has already been mentioned in relationship to confronting. There can't be good, healthy confronting without caring (love). Confronting translates caring into action.

Insight

Nothing takes the place of insight (what Paul calls "discernment" in Phil. 1:9). The ability to discern what is going on in ourselves and others keeps us from needless confronting and helps us deal with the right issues and good timing when we confront.

Initiation

Good confronters can initiate rather than waiting until they are cornered. They are able to initiate at the time when it will do the most good.

Courage

Courage is used to describe the heroic acts of military personnel and the attitude of the critically ill. Courage is needed in everyday life, and especially in confronting others. Revenge and hatred are not the proper emotions for confronting others.

Hope

Good confronting springs from the hope that you can change things for the better. Cynicism poisons confronting. The person who confronts without hope is like a kamikaze pilot seeking only to destroy the other person.

Patience

American journalism seldom praises patience. (Is that because reporters are impatient? They have to get the story by the 6:00 PM news regardless.) Yet patience is an important virtue in confronting. When you confront, it should not be hit-and-run but patiently staying with (emotionally if not physically) the person you confront. If you do not stay with confronting after you start, you will only reinforce the objectionable behavior.

Whom to Confront

Confront healthy people; they can change. Neurotics need care from specialists. Of course, we may not be able to avoid the conflict unhealthy people create.

You should confront people who keep you from reaching your goals. You may need to confront them in order to reexamine your goals or to solicit their help in reaching your goals.

People may refuse to use your good services—your family, your staff, your church members. Since a part of your role and responsibility is to help them, their refusal calls for confronting.

People who arouse feelings in you invite your confronting. Certainly there are other things to consider. Are the feelings because of their personhood, or are the feelings transferred from other relationships? Are the people healthy? If not, confronting them may not help. Is this the optimum time to confront?

Confront people who want to reach goals. You may serve as a catalyst for them to unlock their God-given gifts.

Reality of Conflict

Confrontation leads to conflict. When one person confronts a second, two wills collide. Values, life-styles, investments, goals, modes of operation, and habits conflict.

Conflict is universal. It is not only human; it is part of the structure of all living organisms. Nature has a food chain. Bodies have "antibodies" to ward off the threat by diseases. Organizations vie for position and power. Historically, conflict has been present since the first presence of humanity; and it has not been limited to humankind. No page of a contemporary newspaper fails to bear witness to conflict, whether the international, national, local, business, or sports section is being read.

Is conflict a part of God's plan or is it demonic? You can't read world history without concluding that the demonic played a part in many conflicts. Names such as Dachau and Auschwitz are twentieth-century testimonies to the demonic. Larry McSwain and Bill Treadwell, who have written a major book on conflict management, say, "Conflict was not God's plan for humanity."[2] I think they are correct in saying that God's plan is one of *shalom* (peace). I question whether peace is the absence of conflict. (If so, wouldn't the tranquilizing pills of Huxley's *Brave New World* be the answer?) The promise of the kingdom of God is the good news of peace coming out of conflict by God's divine providence.

Handling Conflict: A Process

"I didn't expect anything like that to happen. People came out of the woodwork with their swords drawn ready to fight. I don't understand what was so important about the issue." These were a pastor's remarks after a stormy business session at the church. The incident arose as the result of a church committee's recommendation.

Understanding and managing conflict are difficult, especially when we are a party in it. This pastor neither understood nor managed it. An outsider, without an emotional investment in the conflict, might have understood the conflict. The pastor would not likely have understood it unless he had a frame of reference.

Many books have been written about managing conflict. The term "managing conflict" infers that a person can control it and manipulate it toward a desired conclusion. I suspect that conflict management is a term that promises too much in a voluntary, democratic institution. I prefer a less grandiose term such as "handling conflict."

There is a process to use in conflict situations. The process also helps us to understand it, even when we can do little about it. The process helps us to handle conflict. Even if we can't control it, we may be able to nudge the conflict in a certain direction, gain some control, or at least understand what is happening.

Anticipate Conflict

Ozark folklore says, "Don't borrow trouble." That doesn't mean for us not to be prepared for it. Every action we take may cause conflicts. People have been crushed because they weren't emotionally prepared to deal with the conflicts they had to face. Anticipate the possibility of conflicts and get yourself emotionally ready to respond. When surprised by a conflict, we may experience a flash of anger and say things which should never be said. We may claim a position too soon or one which is untenable.

Developing Good Attitudes

One reason to anticipate conflict is to develop an appropriate attitude toward conflict. We should believe in the availability and desirability of a mutually acceptable solution. There may not be a solution, but we won't find it without such an attitude.

We need to trust cooperation rather than competition. Western society is so competitive that cooperation is a learned attitude rather than a natural one.

Everyone is of equal value. A person may be wrong about a particular issue, but he or she is made in the image of God and deserves our respect.

People have a right to their opinions. The views of others present are the legitimate statements of their positions.

A good attitude recognizes that differences of opinion are helpful. They enrich proposals. They clarify suggestions.

We must believe in the trustworthiness of others. Many people have opposed my ideas, but I have not found a person who wasn't trying to do what is best; no one has tried to destroy the church but to help it.

Dangers to Avoid

The temptation is to surround ourselves with "yes men" (and women). That only isolates us from conflict temporarily. People really do disagree with you, and you need to hear them. Anticipate the disagreement rather than insulating yourself from it.

Another trap is emphasizing loyalty and cooperation so as to make disagreement sound like disloyalty and rebellion. When you anticipate conflict, you need to hear and honor various opinions and emphasize that people can disagree and still be a part of the team.

As we anticipate conflict, we may succumb to the temptation of "pouring oil on troubled waters." When people feel keenly about an issue, this makes them feel "put down." A storm finally breaks through oil. Glossing over differences does not bring harmony.

Ambiguous resolution of difficulties only puts off the day of reckoning. Later people will feel betrayed when their position is discounted.

Cutting others down to strengthen your position is a time bomb. Divide and conquer is a technique to use in war on enemies, not a process to be used with people who are a part of a team or fellowship. Depersonalize dissent rather than saying, "That's just old George."

Don't jump to conclusions. Listen with understanding rather than evaluation. Others want to be heard and deserve that dignity. They may have something to say, or it may be enough for them to know that they have been heard. Conflict is a time when relationships are vulnerable. It is an occasion to give attention to maintaining good relationships—with dissenters and supporters.

Do's and Don'ts

Precondition yourself emotionally for conflict. Conflict is a time not to forget tenderness toward others. You also need an inner toughness.

Don't get caught crying "wolf." Leaders who use every conflict to claim people are after them find that people eventually don't believe them.

Don't create more crises trying to settle this one. Conflicts improperly resolved breed more conflicts.

Communicate real crises to responsible people. You can't go it alone. Anticipate the help you will need in a conflict and seek it.

Don't fight a battle over you. You may win a battle, but you will lose the war.

Analyze

Schools teach ministers to read books; they also need to learn to read situations. Effective leaders have good powers of analysis. This is a critical step in handling conflict. The leader needs to identify several things to deal with conflict constructively.

The Nature of the Conflict

The conflict may be personal or systemic. According to Speed Leas and Paul Kittlaus, there are three kinds of conflict: intrapersonal, interpersonal, and substantive.[3] The intrapersonal is a struggle within oneself. Interpersonal conflict is not primarily about issues but about differences between people. Substantive conflict is over issues, methods, goals, or values.

The effective leader will find the real issue in conflict and deal with it. The issue at hand may only be a smoke screen. There is no use wasting time over the right plans when the dispute is between the Hatfields and McCoys. The first question is, "What is the real issue?" and it may not be the apparent agenda.

When you deal with the nature of conflict, you will have to determine if it is from reality or fantasy. Is the issue a projection of someone's fears or dreams? Does the conflict come out of history or present reality?

The Source of the Problem

The problem may be logistical; and if you can change the delivery system, you resolve the conflict. The problem may be informational, and you can deal with it by letting everyone know the facts. The problem may be a clash of values. This conflict may only yield to people having greater values which hold them together. It may be a status problem. Some people may feel disenfranchised and will create conflict regardless of what the issue is.

Look at where the conflict originates. Such analysis will tell you where you have to go to solve it.

Where does the conflict come from? Is the source one group or several? Is there interaction between the source of conflict and any other groups? Are there key people in the group which is the source of the conflict? Identify the source of conflict and you may have a means to handle it.

The Depth of Conflict

Conflict is greater when people care. People may politely vote for a resolution about Uganda but fight vehemently about dividing a Sunday School class into two classes.

There is greater conflict over a principle than a person. Sometimes a person is involved, but the real issue which stirs people is the right to deal with a person or the indignities imposed on a person.

People become more excited over an issue that deals with the total life than one which is only about an episode.

When the conflict is a surface issue, it may not become a great threat as long as it is dealt with and the people involved are treated with dignity. An issue which has become complex, threatening principles or a way of life, makes greater demands.

Dynamics of Conflict

No two conflicts are alike; each has its own set of dynamics. The analysis includes sorting out these dynamics and rechecking them from time to time.

Control is one of the dynamics. Who controls the system is im-

Community
Other Churches
Disentrachised Members
Non-Active Members
Specific Age Group
Worshippers
Volunteer Staffs
Deacons
Staff
Pastor

Figure 1

portant. Do you? Does someone else? In a large bureaucracy, the system begins to control the system. Sometimes the system gets out of control and no one is in charge.

There are needs to be met. These may be financial, work, or personal needs.

People make investments. When they give money or work in a church, people are making investments. Families may be the emotional heirs of generations of investments. These determine their responses in conflict.

There may be decisions to be made. The nature and timing of the decisions are part of the dynamics as well as who should make them.

The Term of the Conflict

The conflict may be long term. Is it related to a chronic problem or is it built into the system? The conflict may be situational and therefore short term. You will handle long-term conflicts differently than short-term ones. You need to determine if the term of the conflict is related to a crisis, a current condition, a decision which was made (or is about to be made), a person, or the system itself.

The Cost of the Conflict

Every action has its price, so conflict has its cost. The cost may be the resources or opportunities of the church. This cost may outweigh dealing with a conflict issue. The conflict may keep the church from reaching its goal (or it may only be reached by going through conflict).

Relationships may be the cost of conflict. Churches do split and marriages break up. People may no longer trust one another.

Leaders must weigh the cost of conflict on themselves. Every conflict takes its emotional toll. It takes psychic and physical energy to move through a conflict. When a person has multiple conflicts, he or she may have to choose which is the most vital. Conflict may also erode the leader's self-esteem. One myth many live by is that we can get along with everyone. Conflict may prove this untrue.

Which Phase Are You In?

Five phases have been identified in the evolution of a conflict:[4]
1. Anticipation;
2. Conscious but unexpressed differences;
3. Discussion;
4. Open dispute;
5. Open conflict.

A part of the analysis is to see to the point where the conflict has progressed. We can't turn back the clock. Nothing is as deadly as not knowing where we are in conflict.

Consider Alternatives

Charles Keating says that there are three alternatives: avoid, defuse, or reconcile.[5] Perhaps the fourth would be "run over."

Another way of looking at the alternatives is by the win-lose possibilities. Perhaps the most typical way to try to solve conflicts is with a "win-lose approach." The most productive approach is the win-win.

Fred Pryor provides a diagram relating to the win-lose syndrome.[6] (See Figure 2.)

Whenever anyone in a church loses, everyone loses. The leader's job is not polarization but team building. That is why Keating's "reconciling" is important organizationally, just as reconciling is important theologically.

Hersey and Blanchard (Figure 3) illustrated a concept of developing alternatives related to the importance of a conflict issue.[7]

When we start with the attitude that people will cooperate about serious issues, we can succeed at problem solving in conflict.

When we analyze the data and look at the alternative approaches, we will have to decide our style of handling conflict. There are four possibilities: passive, aggressive, passive-aggressive, or assertive.

The passive style person lets things happen without serious intervention. This person passes control of the situation to any person who wishes to solve the problem. This is a laissez-faire style of leadership.

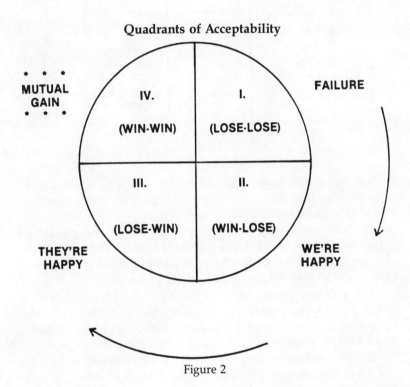

Figure 2

Hersey and Blanchard

Conflict Inevitable, Agreement Impossible	Conflict Not Inevitable, Yet Agreement Not Possible	Although There Is Conflict, Agreement Is Possible	
ACTIVE ↑			**HIGH STAKES** ↑
Win-Lose Power Struggle	Withdrawal	Problem-Solving	
Third-Party Intervention	Isolation	Splitting the Difference (Compromise, Bargaining, etc.) Mediation	**MODERATE STAKES**
Fate	Indifference or Ignorance	Peaceful Coexistence ("Smoothing Over")	
↓ **PASSIVE**			**LOW STAKES** ↓

Figure 3

The aggressive style person runs over any person who gets in the way, leaving tracks on people's backs. This is an autocratic style of leadership.

The passive-aggressive person appears to bend and give in but waits in ambush, perhaps sabotaging the carrying out of a decision or waiting till the next conflict comes along. After sabotage this person may play the game, "See what you made me do?"

The assertive person remains the leader and is intentional in taking action but respects the dignity and rights of others. The assertive person makes the best participative management leader in a conflict situation in a voluntary, democratic organization.

Finally, we have to determine specific alternatives. Make a list of all the alternatives. Include as many ideas of others in each alternative as you can. Let everyone know that you have taken their ideas seriously. Write them out and include the positive benefits and the risks in each. Every alternative will have both.

James Glasse admonishes, "Live to fight another day."[8] We can get so wrapped up in a conflict that we get myopia. When we do, we don't see the larger picture or the long-term effect. We will need our leadership in the future; don't squander everything on one issue. Let the group share the responsibility for the alternatives and decisions.

Decide

"How long halt ye between two opinions?" (1 Kings 18:21, KJV). Elijah was in the midst of conflict with the priests of Baal and called to Israel for a decision. Conflict finally boils down to a decision.

Who decides? That is a crucial question. Sometimes the decision belongs to the staff, sometimes to the congregation. Leaders should not forget their leadership by foregoing the decisions they should make. When a decision has to be made, someone will make it. If the decision belongs to the leader and the leader procrastinates, someone else will make it. Leaders who make a decision that belongs to the congregation will be left to implement the decisions.

Do you need help making the decisions? Several experts have suggested that churches should use consultants when they face decisions in conflict situations. These are not people who make decisions but referees to help churches through processes so the church can come to a decision.

Be careful not to absolutize a decision. It is a temptation in a church. Absolute statements about God and the Bible tend to rub off on church decisions. No decision is perfect. Every decision has pluses and minuses. When you absolutize a decision and a minus appears, you raise the conflict again.

It is my philosophy that every decision is between 40 and 60 percent effective. When a presidential candidate gets 60 percent of the vote, we call it a landslide, but we often demand 100 percent effectiveness. Bernard Baruch (in 1936!) said that if you could guarantee that he would be right 51 percent of the time, he would make a million dollars a day on the stock market (in 1936). Yet we often expect decisions to be 100 percent. We think in absolute terms: right or wrong, good or bad, perfect or useless. A pastor led his congregation to buy a piece of land, saying that it was "God's will." Obviously he put any dissenters in the position of being against God (the game of "Let's you and him fight").

Shortly after the purchase there was a landslide, which not only made the property useless, but brought several lawsuits from neighboring property owners. The pastor lost his leadership.

Implement the Decision

No decision is better than its implementation. Conflict isn't over until there is good implementation. A congregation was divided over building a new sanctuary and then over the architecture. After a beautiful new sanctuary was built and soon paid for, the pastor noted the pride in the *former* critics as they showed *their* new sanctuary to friends.

Implementation should not exclude people who differed during decision making. To exclude them would be to disenfranchise them. The implementation does need to be done by those who have the same goals as the decision calls for. Recently I heard about a group seeking a new executive. They put several people on the search committee who had not supported the group. The process has been chaotic.

The implementation period should be dedicated to the task, not allowing gloating by one group over another group or saying "I told you so." All need to be part of the team. The wise leader will help that happen by attitude and acts.

The Care of People's Needs

An important part of a leader's work in handling conflict is to take care of people's needs at every point in the conflict. Members of the church who are part of the conflict will have pastoral needs. These should be met with intensity and goodwill. People have feelings and these need care. People have emotional investments and these should be cherished.

Respect! That is a key word in handling conflict. Your opponents will support you if you respect them, their ideas, and their feelings. When you are disrespectful of anyone, you alienate your supporters. You are working with God's people, the ambassadors of Christ. Treat them with dignity.

Confrontation and conflict are part of a leader's job. Every job has its challenging side and its shadow side. As a leader, you have to take the whole job.

Notes

1. David Augsburger, *Caring Enough to Confront* (Glendale, Calif.: Regal Books, 1976), p. 176.

2. Larry L. McSwain and William C. Treadwell, Jr., *Conflict Ministry in the Church* (Nashville: Broadman Press, 1981), pp. 19, 202.

3. Speed Leas and Paul Kittlaus, *Church Fights* (Philadelphia: Westminster Press, 1973), pp. 29-35, 186.

4. These are taken from material prepared by the Church Administration Department of the Sunday School Board of the Southern Baptist Convention, 1971.

5. Charles Keating, *The Leadership Book* (Ramsey, N.J.: Paulist Press, Rev. Ed., 1982), pp. 45-47.

6. Fred Pryor Seminars, "Winning Through Negotiation," p. 4. For more information: Fred Pryor Seminars, 2000 Johnson Drive, Shawnee Mission, Kansas 66205.

7. Hersey and Blanchard, p. 287. Their formulation was based on assumptions of Robert Blake, Herbert Shepard, and June Moulton in the book *Managing Intergroup Conflict*.

8. James Glasse, *Putting It Together in the Parish* (Nashville: Abingdon, 1972), p. 37.

Epilogue

Integrity in Working with People

Integrity is a key to working with people. Good leadership demands integrity. Leadership with integrity is not manipulative. I took a group of students to the Kansas City Exchange Building where millions of bushels of grain are bought and sold each day. We watched people buying and selling in the "pit." Our host explained that the Exchange members bought or sold in the "pit" and at the end of the day added up their purchases and sales, regardless of the change of price. One student asked the obvious question, "What if the price went down after they bought and they claimed they didn't buy?" Our host said, "They would never do that." That is integrity at the stock exchange.

We as leaders have ways of showing integrity, too. One is that we need to be concerned with both tasks and persons. The tasks must be real ones. Our concern for people is to help them grow. We are not to burn them out or make them cynical but to help them become what God intended them to be.

The integrity of a leader demands commitment and grace. We must be committed to the kingdom of God, the gospel, and the church. We need to be the bearers of grace to others showing concern, kindness, and even forgiveness.

"Do unto others as you would have them do unto you." The Golden Rule is a clear statement of what integrity means.

Integrity is serving. We are called to be servants, not lords. The integrity of our calling is to serve God and others rather than to demand status.

When we work more effectively with people, we will provide the structure to work and concern for those who work alongside us. This is integrity—and the message of this book.

Bibliography

Augsburger, David. *Caring Enough to Confront*. Glendale, Calif.: Regal Books, 1976.

Berne, Eric. *Games People Play*. New York: Grove Press, 1964.

Blake, Robert R. and Mouton, Jane S. *The New Managerial Grid*. Houston: Gulf Publishing Co., 1978.

Brown, Jerry. *Church Staff Teams that Win*. Nashville: Convention Press, 1979.

Boyle, John. "The Theology of Interpersonal Relationships." *Search*, Summer, 1971.

Bolton, Robert. *People Skills*. Englewood Cliffs, N.J.: Prentice Hall.

Clemons, Hardy. "Building the Team Spirit." *Church Administration*, Sept. 1977.

Clinebell, Howard J., Jr. and Clinebell, Charlotte H., *The Intimate Marriage*. New York: Harper & Row, 1970.

Coleman, Lucien. "How to Put a Part-time Staff Together." *ABC's of Church Administration: How to Work with Church Teachers* (Nashville: Convention Press, 1973).

Cooper, James. *Avoiding Defective Covenants Between the Pastor and the Church*. *Search*, Fall, 1977.

Dale, Robert. *Growing a Loving Church*. Nashville: Convention Press, 1974.

_____. *To Dream Again*. Nashville: Broadman, 1981.

Davis, Keith. *Human Behavior at Work*, 4th ed. New York: McGraw-Hill, 1972.

Elder, Lynn. "The Church as a Complex of Interpersonal Relationships." *Search*, Summer, 1971.

Greenleaf, Robert K. *Servant Leadership*. Ramsey, N.J.: Paulist Press, 1977.

Harbuck, Don. "Creating a Church Staff Team." *Search*, Fall 1974.

Haworth, Swan. "How Church Staff Members Relate." *The Church Musician*, April 1972.

Hersey, Paul and Blanchard, Kenneth. *Management of Organizational Behavior* Englewood Cliffs, N.J.: Prentice Hall, 1982.

Howe, Reuel. *The Miracle of Dialogue*. New York: The Seabury Press, 1963.

James, Muriel and Jongeward, Dorothy. *Born to Win*. Reading, Mass.: Addison-Wesley Publication Co., 1971.

Jones, John. "A Model of Group Development," *1973 Annual Handbook for Group Facilitators*.

Jourard, Sidney. *The Transparent Self*. New York: Van Nostrand, Reinhold Co., 1964.

Judy, Marvin. *The Multiple Staff Ministry*. Nashville: Abingdon, 1969.

Kane, Thomas. *The Healing Touch of Affirmation*. Whitensville: Affirmation Books, 1976.

Keating, Charles. *Dealing with Difficult People*. Ramsey, N.J.: Paulist Press, 1984.

———. *The Leadership Book*. Ramsey, N.J.: Paulist Press, 1982.

Leas, Speed and Kettlaus, Paul. *Church Fights*. Philadelphia: Westminister Press, 1973.

Leslie, Robert. "Developing Interpersonal Relationships Through Small Groups in the Church." *Search*, Summer 1971.

Levinson, Harry. "A Psychologist Looks at Executive Development." *Paths Toward Personal Progress: Leaders Are Made Not Born*. *Harvard Business Review*, 1983, p. 56.

Luft, Joseph. *Group Process*. Palo Alto, Calif.: National Press, 1963.

McDonough, Reginald. *Working with Volunteer Leaders in a Church*. Nashville: Broadman Press, 1976.

McGinnis, Alan. *The Friendship Factor*. Minneapolis: Augsburg Press, 1979.

———. "Research Report—Motivation of Volunteer Workers." *Search*, Summer 1971.

McGee, L. L. "Open Communication." *Search*, Summer 1971.

McSwain, Larry L. and Treadwell, William C., Jr. *Conflict Ministry in the Church*. Nashville: Broadman Press, 1981.

Marney, Carlyle. *Priests to One Another*. Valley Forge, Pa.: Judson Press, 1974.

Maslow, Abraham. *Motivation and Personality*. New York: Harper & Row, 1954.

Mitchell, Kenneth K. *Psychological and Theological Relationships in Multiple Staff Ministry*. Philadelphia: Westminster, 1966.

Oates, Wayne. "Factors Hindering Effective Staff Relationships," *Search*, Summer 1971.

O'Connor, Elizabeth. *Our Many Selves*. New York: Harper & Row, 1971.

Oden, Thomas, *Game Free*. New York: Harper & Row, 1975.

Pattison, E. Mansell. *Pastor and Parish—A Systems Approach*. Philadelphia: Fortress Press, 1977.

Pepper, Kenneth. "Case Study 1: Defective Covenants," *Search*, Summer 1971.

Reddin, William. *Managerial Effectiveness*. New York: McGraw-Hill, 1970.

Riesman, David; Glazier, Nathan; Howe, Reuel. *The Lonely Crowd*. New Haven, Conn.: Yale University Press, 1950.

Satir, Virginia. *People Making*. Science and Behavior Books, Palo Alto, 1972.

Siler, Mahan. "The Growth Spread: A Model for Pastoral Intervention," Department of Pastoral Care, North Carolina Baptist Hospital, Winston-Salem.

Stepsis, Joan. "Conflict-Resolution Strategy, *1974 Annual Handbook for Group Facilitators*, La Jolla.

Sullivan, Henry Stack. *Interpersonal Theory of Psychiatry*. New York: Norton, 1953.

Wedel, Leonard. *Building and Maintaining a Church Staff*. Nashville: Broadman, 1967.

Wright, Richard. *The Outsider*. New York: Harper and Row, 1969.